WONDER
DOGS

WONDER DOGS

First published as *Dog Heroes* in 2009

An Hachette UK Company
www.hachette.co.uk

Summersdale Publishers Ltd
Part of Octopus Publishing Group Limited
Carmelite House
50 Victoria Embankment
LONDON
EC4Y 0DZ
UK

www.summersdale.com

Printed and bound by CPI Group (UK) Ltd, Croydon, CR0 4YY

ISBN: 978-1-84953-997-5

Substantial discounts on bulk quantities of Summersdale books are available to corporations, professional associations and other organisations. For details contact general enquiries: telephone: +44 (0) 1243 771107 or email: enquiries@summersdale.com.

Disclaimer
All stories not directly contributed have been researched from sources in the public domain. Every effort has been made to ensure that all information and any quoted matter in these stories is correct. Should there be any omissions or errors in this respect we apologise and shall be pleased to make the appropriate amendments in any future edition.

WONDER
DOGS

TRUE STORIES
of CANINE COURAGE

BEN HOLT

summersdale

CONTENTS

7   *Introduction*

8   Chapter 1: Taking the Plunge

26   Chapter 2: Protecting Loved
Ones from Human Attacks

40   Chapter 3: A Nose for Rescue

58   Chapter 4: Helping Humans Under Animal Attack

71   Chapter 5: Helping Other Animals in Distress

84   Chapter 6: Helping People

107   Chapter 7: When Disaster Strikes

121   Chapter 8: Dogs of War

135   Chapter 9: Sounding the Alarm

152   Chapter 10: Keeping the Streets Safe

169   Chapter 11: Survivors!

186   *Acknowledgements*

187   *Useful Resources and Information*

INTRODUCTION

For many of us, our dogs are our best friends, helping us through the hard times ('grief busters', as one bereaved woman described them), loving us unconditionally and willing to put their own lives on the line to protect us. Whether they are expensive pedigree dogs, they have been trained to carry out dangerous duties in a war zone, or they have been rescued from a miserable life on the streets, the bond that they have with their humans can be touchingly strong and characterised by a deep devotion and steadfast loyalty.

The true stories in this book, drawn from a wide variety of different situations all around the world, all reflect these qualities in one way or another and clearly show the intelligence, compassion and selflessness inherent in dogs. The courageous canines featured here show their true colours through acts such as leaping into dangerous waters to rescue someone who is drowning, by knowing instinctively that there is a fellow creature in peril and getting help, by risking their life to lead firefighters through a burning building to their trapped loved ones – and through countless other heroic deeds done not for glory or gain, but simply because they are Wonder Dogs!

CHAPTER 1

TAKING THE PLUNGE

Some breeds of dog, such as Labradors and golden retrievers, are natural-born swimmers, while others – such as bulldogs, boxers, greyhounds and Dobermann pinschers – are distinctly not!

As the selection of stories in this section on water rescues shows, however, it's not its degree of affinity for water that determines whether a dog will risk its life to save a drowning person – or even drowning animals – it's the instinctive drive that many dogs seem to possess to help other creatures in distress.

Although many of the stories here feature Labradors, retrievers and other breeds that are comfortable in water, others are about loyal pets of indiscriminate breed who are determined, whatever the cost to themselves, to save their owners from danger.

WHIZZ

Measuring more than six feet tall when standing on his hind legs, Whizz the heroic Newfoundland left giant shoes to fill when he passed away in 2016 after a lifetime spent working in water rescue, as well as enriching the lives of sick children and adults...

After a frantic but fruitless search of the area after one of her red setters, Topper, went missing on a walk, Charlotte Burroughs was lucky enough to bump into David Pugh and his Newfoundland, Whizz. When she asked David if he'd seen Topper along the way, Whizz took off without hesitation for the local water treatment plant, where Topper was floundering around in the water, unable to get out and in grave danger of drowning. Whizz dragged him out, to Charlotte's eternal gratitude.

But this was by no means Whizz's first rescue. Over the course of a decade, the 12-stone hero – a true gentle giant – had rescued nine people from drowning as he patrolled the Bristol Channel and the River Severn with the Royal Navy Rescue, the Severn Area Rescue Association and Marine Volunteer Service. Among those he saved were two small girls who got into trouble in their inflatable dinghy on the Welsh coast and a woman who suffered an asthma attack whilst swimming in the Bristol Channel. He also worked as a therapy dog, visiting the sick and elderly as well as injured servicemen and women.

Whizz was awarded the PDSA Order of Merit – the animal equivalent of an OBE – for outstanding devotion to duty in March 2016.

Sadly he passed away at the age of 12 just before receiving the award, which was presented posthumously, and received on his behalf by Whizz's cousin Tizz and owner David Pugh, who said:

> *I am bursting with pride for Whizz. He was a dog in a million and I am truly heartbroken that he isn't here to receive his medal. Whizz loved working and had an extraordinary talent. Not only was he strong and gentle, he was also so emotionally intuitive. This made him the perfect rescue and therapy dog and a beloved companion to the hundreds of sick children and adults he met along the way.*

BEAR

A little boy is found floating in the swimming pool, seemingly lifeless – but thanks to the family's pet dog, all is not lost...

When 14-month-old Stanley vanished from his mother Patricia's sight in the back garden of their Michigan, USA house in June 2012, her worst fears were realised when she found him floating in the family pool face-up and still.

'It was scary,' Patricia said later. 'His lips were blue. His eyes were rolled back. It was the scariest feeling and the image stays in your head for a long time.'

But as she rushed over to the pool, she saw that the family's black Labrador, Bear, was standing beneath her son and propping him up in an attempt to keep his head out of the water.

'[Bear] wouldn't move in the pool. He didn't bark. It was like he was afraid to move at all until I got Stanley up out of the pool and that's when [Bear] came up out of the pool with me.'

After pulling Stanley out of the water, his mother was unable to get any signal on her phone when she tried calling the emergency services, so she bundled her other children into the car and drove her unresponsive son to the hospital. On the way there, he regained consciousness, bringing up the water he had ingested, and by the time they arrived at the local fire department in Marcellus, Michigan, he was 'alert and in good condition'.

Meanwhile, Bear had instantly become the family hero. 'We all believe that if it wasn't for Bear, [Stanley] would have sunk down. It was incredible to see Bear holding him up like that,' said Patricia, who added that she'd always trained him to look after her young family.

'I've always told Bear growing up, ever since he was a pup to just watch over his babies.'

SWANSEA JACK

The black Labrador retriever dubbed 'Swansea Jack' made as many as 27 watery rescues during his short life in the 1930s...

Jack lived with his owner William Thomas at Padley Yard, Wales, on the western bank of the River Tawe, an area that was made derelict after Swansea's shipping industry shifted to the eastern side of the river.

In 1931, aged just one, the Labrador retriever made his first heroic rescue when a 12-year-old boy who was playing on the wharf fell into the water. As a puppy Jack had always been frightened of deep water (perhaps that would explain why he was so watchful of humans in the river), but as soon as he saw that the boy was in trouble he jumped in and dragged him back to the shallows, where the boy struggled ashore. Despite his timely action, Jack's bravery was not reported at the time.

Several weeks later, Jack performed a second successful rescue by saving a flagging swimmer from the nearby waters of North Dock. This time his actions attracted a small crowd, and his photo and an account of the rescue were printed in the local newspaper. He was awarded a silver collar by the city council for his efforts, and sprang to fame as a local hero.

By the age of five, Jack had made so many rescues that he was featured in the national newspapers. He won numerous accolades for his service to humans, including two bronze stars from the National Canine Defence League, the 'Bravest

Dog of the Year' award from both *The Star* newspaper and the *Daily Mirror* in 1936, and the 'Bravest Dog' category at Crufts. He was even presented with a silver cup by the Lord Mayor of London when he was taken on a nationwide tour. Later, Jack also helped to raise substantial amounts of money for charitable causes when his owner permitted the famous and wealthy to be photographed with him.

Sadly, on 2 October 1937, aged just seven, Jack died after accidentally eating rat poison. A memorial to this charismatic and courageous canine was erected near to his favourite swimming spot on the promenade in Swansea, near St Helen's Rugby Ground. It can still be visited today.

MAGGIE

A dramatic river rescue was just one of the ways in which Maggie the golden retriever displayed the amazing bond she had with the little girl who had given her a loving new home...

There was no question in two-year-old Taylor Morgan's mind as to which dog she and her family would rescue the day they went to the local animal shelter. The toddler went straight over to a golden retriever sitting quietly in her cage and said to her, 'Hello Maggie, we are taking you home.'

In return, Maggie would go on the save Taylor's life twice in ways that showed the strength of the incredible bond that had developed between dog and child.

On the first occasion, the usually calm and quiet dog burst into the house through the screen door barking frantically, and when Taylor's parents rushed out into the back garden to find out what had upset the dog, they discovered that Taylor had been stung on the neck by a bee and was having a severe allergic reaction, causing her to have difficulty breathing.

The second rescue came two years later, in the form of a dramatic dive into the Lewis River in the family's home state of Washington, USA, after Taylor slipped and fell into the raging torrent that the river had become following heavy rain. As soon as Taylor, then six years old, fell in, Maggie had darted down the bank and leapt into the river ahead of Taylor, who was by now underwater. The next thing Taylor's frantic parents saw was Maggie emerging from under the water with Taylor gripped in her teeth by her jacket. The pair were swept another hundred yards downriver before Maggie was able to drag the child to the bank. Tom, Taylor's father, then grabbed her jacket, and between him and Maggie they dragged her onto the grass and safety.

'Even though they went under a few times she didn't let go once. If it hadn't been for Maggie, we would have lost our daughter,' said a grateful Tom.

Taylor explained the river rescue by simply saying, 'Maggie loves me.'

Sergeant Michael Brodie, the policeman who dealt with the incident, said, 'I have never heard of a dog jumping into a river to save a child before. The family is very lucky to own a dog with this degree of devotion. When I took the report at the family's home, the dog sat there looking back and forth between me and Taylor and I could sense something extremely unusual between them.'

Tom said, 'We have always known there was an unusual bond between them. When Taylor was younger and first walking, Maggie would move toys out of her path and always sleeps just outside her bedroom door as if on guard.'

Sadly, Maggie was diagnosed with an aggressive form of cancer that would take her life a few months after the second rescue – but not before she received a nomination by the police department for a Commendation of Bravery for her courageous and dramatic river rescue of the little girl who was the love of her life.

BILBO

Bilbo was a 14-stone chocolate brown Newfoundland who lived with his owner near Land's End in Cornwall, UK. What started out as a natural love for the water resulted in Bilbo becoming the world's first qualified surf lifeguard dog, credited with saving several lives…

Bilbo's owner, Steve Jamieson (known as Jmo), was the head lifeguard at Sennen Cove, a beach near their home. When Bilbo first came to live with him, Jmo understood the famous Newfoundland reputation for an affinity with water. Bilbo absolutely loved the water, and when he went to the beach with Jmo he enjoyed playing in the waves and swimming with the lifeguards.

After a while, Jmo realised that Bilbo could be a useful addition to the lifeguarding team at Sennen Cove and decided to train him to help out. Bilbo had to be put through the same swimming and fitness tests as the other lifeguards and learn how to swim in all types of sea conditions. He was soon swimming with skill and confidence and became a fully-fledged member of the team – the world's first fully qualified surf lifeguard dog. But Jmo had also come up with a unique way of using Bilbo to help get the safety message across to beachgoers:

> We [the lifeguards] were then employed by the local council who had spent thousands of pounds producing sea safety signs advising the public about beach safety, the flag system and so on. Hardly anyone took any notice of these signs. I had an idea to have a coat made for Bilbo in red and yellow – the same colour as the flags we want bathers to swim between. It would also have the message 'swim between the flags' on it. When Bilbo went on patrol he would wear his coat, becoming an instant success with the public.

As dogs are not allowed on the beach in the summer, Bilbo was driven around on the back of a quad bike across the beach, watching for bathers in trouble. The quad stopped at intervals so that everyone could meet Bilbo and read the message on his lifejacket. The lifeguards also patrolled on a motorised rescue ski; Bilbo rode on the sled at the back, from which he could leap off into the sea to assist struggling swimmers and tow them back to safety. Jmo organised regular demonstrations where Bilbo simulated rescues to illustrate the dangers of swimming in strong currents.

We trained Bilbo to recognise when someone was in trouble in the sea, waving and shouting for help. Bilbo wears a harness under his coat onto which we would clip a buoyancy aid. He would, on locating the 'casualty', swim out through the surf, towing the tube behind him. He would then swim around the casualty, drawing the float close to them. When he felt their weight clutching the tube he would turn and tow them ashore.

Perhaps Bilbo's distinguishing skill, though, was his ability to warn people of imminent danger in the water. One woman had changed into her swimming things in a remote cove and was heading into the water. Jmo advised her against going in, explaining that the currents had recently shifted and were extremely dangerous, but she ignored him and headed towards the water anyway.

Jmo described what happened next: 'Without any prompting whatsoever, Bilbo sensed that she was going to get into the sea, and he simply took off spontaneously and ran back down the cliff path towards the woman on the beach, placing himself between her and the sea, actually standing on her feet. She shouted to me to call the dog off, but Bilbo would not move. However, the woman pushed past Bilbo, whereupon he raced into the surf to block her way. Only then did she realise how strong the current was, as she saw what a difficult time Bilbo was having in the powerful waves, so she did not go in.'

Bilbo's intuition and perseverance had prevented the woman from getting into trouble and being swept away by the strong currents surrounding the cove that day.

His bravery did not go unrecognised and the local and national press ran coverage of the story – Bilbo even appeared on national television.

Alongside his regular lifeguarding duties, Bilbo toured schools with Jmo, teaching children about beach safety and making sure they remembered to 'swim between the flags'. He became something of a celebrity and received fan mail and presents from people all over the world. With over 250,000 people visiting Sennen's mile-long beach every year, Bilbo certainly had an important task on his hands in educating the beachgoers – and he seemed to manage to put a smile on everyone's face while doing it!

Sadly, in May 2015 Bilbo passed away. Jmo posted on Facebook: 'Just to let you know that my lovely, lovely Bilbo/ Best Friend/Saviour, slipped his moorings late this afternoon and has sailed off without me. R.I.P Bilbo, Gwynver supreme 2003–2015.'

WHAT MADE BILBO A GOOD SURF LIFEGUARD DOG?

Bilbo was a Newfoundland, a dog breed originating in Newfoundland in Canada that is perfectly adapted to cope with the water. They have a double coat: oily and waterproof on top, and fine-haired underneath for warmth and insulation. Their long, powerful legs give them extra swimming strength and their large, webbed paws act like paddles. With a broad, strong tail that acts as a rudder, ears that stick flat to the head when in the water to prevent liquid getting in, and a large lung capacity that gives them increased endurance, these dogs are excellent candidates for lifeguard training and have been credited with many rescues.

YARON

Guide dog Yaron astonished everyone one summer by acting above and beyond his guide dog duties to rescue a little girl from danger...

Jon Hastie was on holiday with his brother, his brother's wife and their two young daughters on the Isles of Scilly, UK. Yaron, Jon's black Labrador-golden retriever cross, came along to fulfil his usual duties of safely guiding his blind owner.

The family were spending the afternoon at the beach when Jon's niece Charlotte, aged seven, fell off her bodyboard into the sea. She quickly started to drift out of her depth and, despite the fact that she was wearing a life jacket, became increasingly distressed. She tried to grab hold of her bodyboard and get back on, but in her panic she splashed around, which pushed the board further away. Jon recounted what happened next:

> *Yaron saw that Charlotte was distressed*
> *and jumped into the sea. He swam out to*
> *Charlotte and began to circle around her,*
> *so that she could grab hold of his collar,*
> *before swimming back to shore. Charlotte's*
> *dad helped to bring them both safely back*
> *to the shore and neither were hurt, just a*
> *bit soggy!*

Yaron's brave and intelligent reaction had prevented the situation from becoming far more serious; he had understood the situation quickly and taken it upon himself to help the distressed girl. After the terrifying ordeal, Charlotte realised the important role Yaron had played in her rescue. Jon described how the little girl expressed her gratitude:

> *Charlotte was over the moon with Yaron,*
> *telling anyone and everyone that he had*
> *saved her life. This isn't what a guide dog*
> *is trained to do but Yaron went beyond*
> *the call of duty and is certainly a winner*
> *to me and my family.*

Yaron was named Beyond the Call of Duty Guide Dog of the Year 2008 as part of the prestigious Guide Dog of the Year Awards. The award was presented by television presenter Peter Purves. Vicky Bell, a spokesperson for the Guide Dogs for the Blind Association, commented, 'It is fantastic that Yaron's bravery has been recognised and we are able to celebrate his amazing achievement.'

ECHO

Echo proved to be an invaluable canoeing companion to her owner on a five-day trip that almost ended in disaster...

As a keen but inexperienced adventurer, Tish Smith of Manitoulin Island, Canada, planned a canoe trip on Lake Huron, the second largest of the North American Great Lakes and the third largest freshwater lake in the world. Echo, her German shepherd–collie mix pet dog, had always seemed at home in the great outdoors and especially loved to swim, so Tish brought her along for company, thinking she would enjoy the trip. They were to spend five days crossing the water, taking in some astonishingly beautiful waterscapes, distant rugged shorelines and dramatic skies. But at 6 a.m. on the final day their lake adventure took a turn for the worse.

Although it was summer, a huge storm suddenly engulfed the area, creating enormous waves that lashed their canoe. Tish tried to put a lifejacket on Echo, but Echo would not cooperate, instead nuzzling up to Tish. Tish spoke constantly to Echo while fighting for hours to keep the canoe upright, but it was eventually capsized by an enormous wave, catapulting them both into the freezing water. They thrashed helplessly in the raging waves as their canoe and everything on board disappeared into the storm.

The pair remained in the water for the next 12 hours, during which time Echo never left her owner's side, providing reassurance to Tish and also helping to keep her warm. 'It was shocking how cold it was for July,' Tish later said. 'We swam around for hours. I thought we'd be OK, but it was so cold.'

Although Tish was a qualified nurse, she was so worried about Echo not wearing a lifejacket that she failed to notice the onset of severe hypothermia in her own body. Suddenly she felt a warm and happy sensation rush over her, as she slipped into unconsciousness.

Luckily, Tish's canoe was discovered and the OPP Marine Search and Rescue Team and the Canadian Air Force Search and Rescue Team from Trenton were called out. Although an initial search found nothing, a crew on an aerial sweep over the area spotted Echo swimming in circles around Tish's floating body.

By the time the pair were found, they had drifted within striking distance of land. A dog's instinct in this situation would have been to swim to the safety of the shore but, in spite of this, Echo remained by Tish's side. Echo's dense coat stopped her own body temperature from dropping to dangerous levels, and the heat she had passed on to Tish slowed the progress of her hypothermia. They were pulled from the water by paramedics and taken to hospital, where Tish made a full recovery.

By refusing to leave Tish, Echo had saved her life twice over – by keeping her core temperature above the survival point and by attracting the attention of rescuers who may not otherwise have spotted Tish in the water. 'Without Echo... there wouldn't have been a rescue,' said Tish, who learned a valuable lesson that day not to underestimate the potential dangers of the great outdoors.

TANG

A Newfoundland called Tang saved 92 people on board a sinking ship off the coast of the region in Canada after which his breed was named...

When a ship crashed into rocks off the coast of Newfoundland, Canada, in the winter of 1919, it took the might of the ship's dog, Tang, to rescue the people on board the doomed ship. One of the crew of the *Ethie* had died trying to swim to shore with one of the ship's ropes, so the captain turned to Tang as his final hope for saving the day.

The dog was able to do what the sailor had died trying to do – swim to shore with the rope in his teeth while the powerful waves crashed around him and pulled him back out. When he eventually managed to reach land, people who had been watching from the shore took the rope from his mouth, tied it up and used it to bring everyone left on the sinking ship – all 92 of them – to safety.

Tang was awarded a medal for his bravery by Lloyds of London, famous as an insurer of ships, and the heroic Newfoundland wore it for the rest of his life.

THE FIRST WATER RESCUE DOG

One of the earliest references to water rescue dogs is an ancient seafaring tale about a spectacular rescue of a drowning sailor by a Newfoundland dog, who pulled the man back onto the boat after he had been swept off the deck during a storm.

The story was the inspiration behind the founding of the Italian School of Rescue Dogs (Scuola Italiana Cani Salvataggio, SICS) in 1989 by Ferruccio Pilenga, together with his Newfoundland dog called Mas. Today it is the largest national organisation dedicated to the training of dogs and their handlers for water rescue. Any breed of dog can undergo training here, though it must weigh more than 30 kilograms and be confident in the water.

The school's high standards and modern techniques revolve around collaborating with the coast guards and studying their use of dinghies, helicopters and sailing and air instruments.

Its training programme's focus is on creating a very strong two-way relationship between dog and handler where both rely on each other:

🐾 Following the rigorous training programme of both dog and handler, with the assistance of the dog the handler will be able to resuscitate a person whilst still in the water.

❧ The training programme develops the dogs' power and stamina to an incredible degree: one dog alone will be able to pull a boat full of 30 people for between 300 and 2,000 metres.

❧ By the end of training, dog and handler will be able to swim side by side in complete synchronisation, essential during a rescue.

❧ A qualification certificate (the SICS) is issued when the required standard is successfully reached.

The Italian School of Rescue Dogs is also the only institution in Europe to organise yearly classes for heli-rescue dogs, and collaborates with the various Italian heli-rescue teams (from Air Rescue, the Air Force, Police, Customs, the Fire Service and Civil Defence).

CHAPTER 2

PROTECTING LOVED ONES FROM HUMAN ATTACKS

This chapter recounts the stories of the brave dogs who selflessly leapt to the defence of humans – sometimes their owners, sometimes people they'd never met before – to save them from a violent situation, often at great risk to their own safety.

Although certain types of dog, such as German shepherds, pit bulls and Staffordshire bull terriers, are bred specifically as guard dogs and are therefore the most likely breeds to attack when they feel threatened, as these stories show, dogs of all kinds are capable of going on the attack in order to defend someone or something they consider to be part of their 'pack' – usually their owner or other people and animals they live with – regardless of the resulting danger to themselves.

ROCKY

When a pregnant woman and her partner were viciously attacked in their own home in Gravesend, UK, late one night by a gang of thugs, their pet Rottweiler Rocky saw the attackers off...

Rocky the Rottweiler had become agitated when there was a knock at the door after his owners, Kasha Marie Weston and her partner Aryan Salhi, had gone to bed. He started barking frantically, so the couple shut him in the bathroom, before peering outside to see who was at their door, and then gently opening it when they could see no one.

At that point a gang of hooded men burst into their flat shouting, 'Where's the money?' While one held a knife to Kasha's throat, the others started punching Aryan.

It was then that Rocky managed to bust his way through the closed bathroom door, chasing the four terrified thugs out of the flat and down the street, joined by Aryan after he had made sure that Kasha was OK.

Kasha followed, to find Aryan holding one of the men. She said: 'He was saying, "I'm sorry," and Rocky was growling. Aryan held on to him and the police arrived. We gave our statements and then made such a fuss of Rocky. Who knew what would've happened if he hadn't been there?'

Although the other three gang members were not caught, 19-year-old Benedict Ayolla was convicted of aggravated burglary and jailed for ten years.

Devoted Rocky didn't leave pregnant Kasha's side for the next few days after the attack.

'He'd even tenderly nudge my bump with his nose. It was as if he was telling the baby not to worry either,' said Kasha.

On 28 July 2012, two months early, and after bleeding thought to have been brought on by the stress of the attack, Kasha gave birth to a baby boy, who was named Aryan after his dad.

'Nobody was happier about our new arrival than Rocky. He would gaze at him in his cot, stood guard and growled if strangers got too close. We called him Aryan's big brother.'

CALAMITY JANE

Although Calamity Jane had lost a leg due to a bullet wound, that didn't deter the gutsy dog from seeing off a group of armed robbers who were terrorising the neighbours...

Calamity Jane, a golden retriever, was discovered abandoned by the side of the road in Texas. Worse, her left front leg had a bullet wound and had to be amputated in order to save her life, and during the emergency surgery she was also found to be pregnant.

The dog was taken into care by Golden Retriever Rescue of North Texas. There, she adapted to life on three legs and gave birth to seven healthy puppies. Life was looking up for Calamity Jane. Or so you might have thought.

Her puppies were just a few weeks old when she somehow sensed trouble nearby. The Koleman family next door were being attacked by armed robbers and held at gunpoint that late January night. An unlikely hero, this three-legged golden retriever started barking at once, causing the robbers to flee – hotly pursued by Calamity Jane, who had good reason to be wary of guns, but wasn't going to be deterred even though she had lost a leg to one.

'Things could have turned out a lot different had it not been for her,' Steven Koleman told a local TV station. The Kolemans credited Calamity Jane with saving their lives.

THE QUALITIES NEEDED FOR A GUARD DOG THAT'S ALSO A FAMILY DOG

Although any dog can be trained for obedience, dogs that are specially trained to protect the family property must have a certain temperament:

- They must be good with all members of the family, especially any children.

- They must get along with any other pets that the family possesses.

- They must have a natural instinct to protect their territory against possible intruders or strangers.

-  They must not be scared of loud noises or any threatening movements made by the intruder.

- They must have an instinct to attack any intruder in their territory – to the point of lifting the intruders' legs off the ground from the force of their impact.

KILLIAN

Out-of-the-ordinary aggressive behaviour from the usually docile family dog saved a little boy from an abusive babysitter...

Killian was a normally calm and friendly black Labrador-German shepherd mix, who belonged to the Jordan family: Benjamin, his wife, and their seven-month-old baby boy Finn, in Charleston, South Carolina, USA. When Killian started growling at the babysitter one day, standing protectively between her and Finn, his hackles rising whenever he was in her presence, it prompted the Jordans to hide an iPhone in the living room to record what went on the next time they left her in charge of little Finn.

To their horror and disbelief, on the recording they could hear 22-year-old Alexis Khan screaming obscenities at their baby and, worse still, noises that sounded like her slapping and shaking him.

Benjamin immediately had his young son checked at the local hospital, where thankfully he was found to be OK. He then contacted the police.

Although they weren't sure that the iPhone recording would be considered sufficient evidence against the young woman, who had been babysitting for them for five months and who had worked in a similar position for numerous other families, in the end she gave a full confession during an interview with the police.

Thanks to Killian's protective behaviour raising the Jordans' suspicions, the abusive babysitter, who pleaded guilty to assault and battery, was sentenced to a maximum of three years in prison and her name included on the child registry, meaning that she would never be permitted to work with children again.

'Who knows how many children she has abused or how many more she would have had it not been for our dog,' said Benjamin. He was so impressed by Killian's protective behaviour towards his son that he has since enrolled him on a training course to be a psychiatric service animal.

A PROTECTIVE PIT BULL

A dog with no name but a fierce loyalty to his family
stepped in to prevent what could have been a tragedy...

He may not have had a name, but a family's pit bull mix knew exactly what he had to do when two armed strangers tried to abduct their baby girl.

A man and woman broke into the family's apartment in Indianapolis, USA in November 2012 and demanded money from Nayeli Garzon-Jimenez, who was on the phone to her husband, Adolfo Angeles-Morales, at the time. Nayeli told her husband that they were threatening to kidnap their daughter if she didn't do what they said.

When she told them she didn't have any money, the woman grabbed Nayeli's three-month-old daughter and made a break for the back door with her.

That was when the family's pit bull cross stepped in, snarling at the would-be kidnapper and preventing her from getting through the door. Terrified, she threw the baby back to the little girl's frantic mother and the pair ran off towards their car. The police put out a detailed description of the couple and their car and immediately launched a hunt to track them down.

Meanwhile, Nayeli was treated for minor injuries as a result of being hit on the head by a gun during the struggle, but her daughter – thanks largely to the family's loyal dog – escaped completely unharmed.

KAISER

Craig Cunningham from Cumbria, UK, who regularly looked after a Staffordshire bull terrier called Kaiser, was protected by the heroic dog when a man approached him and demanded money...

Thirty-one-year-old Craig was out walking his friend Ryan's dog, Kaiser, in Workington when a man wearing a hooded top appeared out of a back alley and demanded money. When Craig said that he didn't have any, the man drew a knife and started wielding it. Kaiser leapt in to defend Craig, putting himself in danger, and the attacker then stabbed Kaiser with the knife.

'Anyone who knows Kaiser knows he's a good little jumper, and when he saw the lad come for me, he jumped in between us... I was really shaken,' said Craig when describing the frightening ordeal.

Unfortunately, the extent of the heroic dog's injuries was only discovered the following morning. By the time he was taken in to the vet's, Kaiser had lost a great deal of blood – six pints, in fact. He was rushed into surgery.

The next hours would determine whether Kaiser had lost his own life while protecting his guardian. Thankfully, he survived, and was returned safely to his owner, Ryan. Craig applauded the dog's heroism, saying, 'He's been a little hero. If it wasn't for Kaiser I'd have been the one to get stabbed.'

MAYA

A peace-loving pit bull cross saved her owner
from a vicious attack in her own home...

Maya the pit bull cross is truly an ambassador for a breed that has acquired an unfortunate – and often unfair – reputation for being unsuitable as pets. Having saved her owner, Angela Marcelino, from an attempted rape in her home in San Jose, California, USA she has well and truly earned the right to be pampered.

'I opened my front door and was about to walk inside when I saw someone's shadow out of the corner of my eye,' Angela explained.

> *I turned my head just as a man pushed me into my house. I screamed as loud as I could, but the man had slammed the door shut behind him. 'Shut up' were the only words he said to me. He was choking me with one hand. I was able to scream one last time. After I did, his grip tightened around my neck. That is when I saw a white streak run in from the other room.*

The white streak was Maya, then five years old and weighing 11 kilograms, who lunged angrily at the man, forcing him to fight her off even though he was still gripping Angela's throat. Maya's attack so startled the man that Angela had the opportunity to grab him in the groin and pull hard. The man doubled over in pain and let go of her, at which point she pushed him away and pulled Maya back in by her collar.

'I like to think, at that moment, he told himself he had picked the wrong woman to mess with. He looked at me one last time, only for a second, and then simply walked away,' said Angela.

The man was later identified through a drop of blood above Maya's right eye and arrested. As for Maya, she proved overwhelmingly that pit bulls are as likely to be hero dogs as any other breed, and in 2008 she was honoured for her bravery by the Animal Miracle Foundation. 'I'm so proud and grateful to have her as part of the family,' said Angela. 'It makes each day a little easier to deal with. We can't imagine life without her.'

PIT BULLS – A DANGEROUS BREED?

The term 'pit bull' is used in reference to several breeds of dog, most commonly the American pit bull terrier, the American Staffordshire terrier and the Staffordshire bull terrier. Pit bulls have a reputation for being aggressive and dangerous, as these animals often fall into the hands of irresponsible people, who may only be interested in owning the dog because of the 'macho image' connected to them. Their bad reputation stems from their history as fighting dogs, and has been worsened by reports in the press of pit bulls that have attacked humans, including small children. In the UK, restrictions have been placed on the ownership of pit bulls under the Dangerous Dogs Act 1991, and some states in the USA have laws restricting breeding and ownership. But as the three stories above show, they can be loyal, loving and highly protective companions, especially if they are trained and handled properly.

GRACIE

Gracie was only a puppy when a violent intruder entered her home and assaulted her owner, but in spite of her young age she acted with astounding speed and effectiveness in combating the attack...

Thirty-two-year-old mother of three Tonya Kendall was at her apartment in Imperial, Missouri, USA with her 11-month-old son playing with his toys on the living room floor, when she heard a knock on the door late one morning.

'Who is it?' she asked.

'Cable guy,' a man answered. Tonya remembered her neighbours talking about the problems they'd had with their cable the week before, so she opened the door.

She was unlucky.

The man pushed his way through the door and knocked her onto the stairs behind, pulled her T-shirt up and began to wrestle with her jeans. She later remembered that he smelled bad, a mixture of car engines and body odour, and was wearing a cap and a sweatshirt with the hood pulled over his face. But it was exposed as he held his gloved hand over her mouth.

Tonya was unable to move, but suddenly she saw her young dog Gracie appear at the top of the stairs above her. The 50-pound German shepherd puppy lunged down the stairs at the man, landing on his shoulder and clamping its teeth into his flesh.

The attacker stood up and threw the puppy across the room. Tonya was devastated and frightened. Gracie, however, was determined and undeterred. She charged again, this time locking on the man's right arm.

Again, he shook himself free and flung the dog back across the living room. But he wasn't waiting around for a third attack. As the dog came towards him again, he retreated out the door – with a threat.

'That's all right. I'll be back to finish what I started.'

Tonya locked the door behind her attacker and at once grabbed her young child. She also found a baseball bat and a knife for self-protection. Then she sat down to telephone the police and her fiancé.

A knock at the door made her jump up with a start. Was her attacker back already? Would he be so bold as to force his way in again, knowing that she could easily identify him, having seen his face? Mercifully, it wasn't him: it was the police.

The detectives with the Jefferson County Sheriff's Department showed her their badges and she described her attacker to a sketch artist – eyebrows, hair, eyes and any distinguishing features. The drawing, when completed, made her physically sick, such was the trauma she had endured.

'It was him, in my house, all over again,' she said. 'But I can't completely fall apart. I've got three children. This man is not going to ruin my life. He's not. I won't let him.'

That night, tossing and turning, Tonya imagined she could still smell the attacker in the room, although her fiancé assured her she was safe. Then, sensing her need for further reassurance, someone else climbed in beside her too. Having selflessly and heroically saved her owner from a vicious attacker earlier that day, Gracie now became the soothing presence Tonya needed to fall into a healing sleep.

DOGS OF VALOR

The Humane Society of the United States created the Dogs of Valor Awards to give recognition to dogs that have performed an extraordinary act of courage by heroically helping a person in need. In 2012, the winner of the fifth annual award and the People's Hero was Hank, owned by McKenzie of Kansas City, Missouri.

After McKenzie's boyfriend threw her through a wall and hit her with a hammer in a fit of rage, Hank, McKenzie's young Great Dane, crawled on top of her to shield her from the blows. The attacker then turned on Hank, shattering his ribs and a hip and then dragging the seriously injured dog onto a busy street and leaving him for dead. He returned to the house, where he told McKenzie that if she called Hank he would shoot them both. McKenzie managed to escape and made her way to a police station, pursued by her attacker with a gun. McKenzie and Hank were treated for their injuries and were reunited at an emergency shelter for victims of violent families.

As a direct result of Hank's bravery and the inspiring love that he and McKenzie shared, the shelter that took them in now provides facilities enabling any domestic violence survivors in a similar situation, with beloved pets that they are desperate to hold on to, to keep them with them.

CHAPTER 3

A NOSE FOR RESCUE

For centuries people have been training and breeding dogs to locate missing people by using their sense of smell and their sense of direction – both of which are far superior to those of humans. The St Bernard, originally kept by monks in the Alps for winter rescue and credited with saving thousands of lives, is one of the most famous type of rescue dog.

Air-scenting dogs increase the efficiency of search teams, enabling them to quickly cover large areas of ground. These dogs are trained to return to their handler as soon as they have found the target, give them a special 'alert' signal, and then lead them back to the target, often an injured person.

Large, strong and agile breeds that have a keen sense of smell, such as German shepherds, golden retrievers and Belgian Malinois, are particularly well suited to this type of work, that often takes place in difficult and dangerous conditions. But, as the selection of stories in this chapter shows, there are also instances of untrained and self-appointed 'rescue' dogs following their noses and their natural instincts to bring an endangered person to safety.

GLORY

When an experienced bloodhound got on the
scent of a lost pet, the missing animal's owners
could rest easy in the knowledge that they had one
of the best noses in the business on the job!

Glory, a bloodhound with a wealth of experience tracking hundreds of lost pets, was deservedly a finalist in the 2015 American Humane Association Hero Dog Awards. She has found many beloved animals that have gone missing, often working in extreme temperatures and under very difficult conditions.

Glory correctly indicated that Pistol the cat had crossed a busy freeway in California, USA – to her owners' astonishment. But she was quickly reunited with her distraught owners once Glory got on her trail.

But Goldie was one of Glory's most spectacular finds. Goldie was a beloved Pekingese who had been lost by a pet-sitter when, without seeking the family's permission, he had taken her to the city where he worked, over 60 miles away from her home. Spooked by a noise, the Pekingese had darted and backed out of her collar, and had then run away.

'It was more than my family could bear. Our hearts were broken,' said family member Karin.

They had spent a week searching unsuccessfully for their beloved pet, putting up 300 posters, offering a thousand-dollar reward, and calling out her name through a megaphone. To their relief, Glory and her handler Landa arrived on the scene on day eight.

Twenty-four hours of non-stop work later, in the driving rain, the bloodhound tracked down the little dog under a pile of crates outside a factory, to the family's immense relief and gratitude. They would feel forever indebted to the wonder dog who, after nine days of torment, had brought their beloved pet back to them.

HOLLY

A young, unmanageable bloodhound narrowly escaped death to become a skilled olfactory sleuth...

Holly didn't have the best start in life. The unruly bloodhound had six different owners in her first year of life and was scheduled to be put down due to her uncontrollable behaviour.

Her lucky break came when Larry Allen, who works with rescue dogs as a member of Barbour County Tactical Search and Recovery Teams in West Virginia, USA, stumbled across her and, despite her destructive, troubled nature decided to give the puppy a go, training her as a police tracker dog.

He said:

> *The first time I saw Holly, all I could think was, how am I going to make this puppy into a working dog in twelve weeks? Little did I know that she would develop a love for the game within two weeks and go on to be one of the best trainees I have ever had. The more that I worked with her, the more*

solid she became and the more she became
my partner.

But it was Holly's 'exquisitely designed nose', according to Allen, that made her such a great tracker.

'The working ability of a bloodhound is seventy-five per cent nature and twenty-five per cent nurture,' he says.

After completing the 12-week training, Holly began working in the K-9 corps of the Massachusetts State Police, where she has been involved in life-saving cases involving searching for missing people as well as tracking violent criminals.

Not bad for a dog who nearly didn't make it into adolescence!

DID YOU KNOW?
HOW MUCH A BLOODHOUND
IS LED BY ITS NOSE

Bloodhounds are recognised as being so skilled at tracking scents that results obtained from their use are accepted as admissible evidence in courts of law. They can focus completely on a trail until they have found its source or reached its end, for well over a hundred miles if necessary, even if there are many other odours in the air. They can track scents that are 300 hours old, and to them the 'odour image' that is formed in their brain from the chemical signals created by the scent is far more detailed than a photograph is for a human. Using this odour image, the bloodhoundis able to locate a subject's trail – a chemical cocktail of scents made up of breath, sweat and loose skin cells.

Bloodhounds' entire nasal, facial and bodily design helps them in their drive to sniff out trouble. Their noses have approximately 230 million olfactory cells, or 'scent receptors' – 40 times more than humans have – with a set of scent membranes that are at least a thousand times more sensitive than those of humans. Their olfactory centre is the size of a handkerchief – far bigger even than that of most other breeds of scent dogs, and vastly bigger than humans', which is the size of a postage stamp. Their loose, wrinkled facial skin helps them trap scent particles, while their long, drooping ears collect odours by dragging on the ground and sweeping them into the area of the nostrils. Their long necks and muscular, sloping shoulders allow them to remain close to the ground while they are tracking, for great distances if necessary.

Bloodhounds have worked in law enforcement for more than 200 years. A Kentucky bloodhound born in 1900 called Nick Carter used his nose to help capture and convict more than 600 criminals, and the breed is thought by many experts to be a greater asset to the police than much state-of-the-art high-tech surveillance equipment.

CHARCO

Charco saved a man's life after the Kashmir earthquake in 2005, and was given a hero's welcome when he returned home to the UK...

The Kashmir earthquake of 2005 struck on 8 October, with its epicentre in Pakistan near the border with India. A sniffer-dog rescue team from Llanfairfechan, Wales, known as BIRD (British International Search and Rescue Dogs) was dispatched to work in Muzaffarabad, one of the worst-hit areas. This was as part of a wider 38-strong British rescue team sent to Pakistan.

'We arrived at a row of buildings which looked like they could collapse at any minute,' said Mr Powell, the handler for one of the sniffer dogs, Charco. 'The heat was intense and Charco squeezed into a passage full of rubble. Despite continuing aftershocks, he went to a corner and started barking.'

The team pulled a 20-year-old man from the wreckage following Charco's indication that he had found someone buried beneath the rubble. The man had been trapped for 54 hours and at that stage in the rescue process was one of only two people recovered alive in the area.

His handler, Neil Powell, described how Charco, a nine-year-old black Labrador, had to work in some highly treacherous conditions, but never once refused to complete his duties.

After each of his heroic stints abroad, Charco had to spend six months in quarantine, the first time after assisting at an earthquake in Algeria in 2003, in which more than 2,000 people died. Following his work in Pakistan, Charco's international career was at an end and he returned to Mr Powell's home at the foot of the Mournes, near Newcastle, Co. Down, Northern Ireland. From then on, he would be working on home territory, helping the Fire Service in search and rescue at his home in Northern Ireland. But that didn't bother him.

'Since he has been home, his tail has never stopped wagging,' Mr Powell said at the time.

Charco, who once cut his feet badly at a gas explosion but was desperate to get back to work afterwards, despite the bandages, was shortlisted for The Sun Hero Dog Award, part of the Dogs Trust Honours 2009. He died in 2014 at the age of 15.

DOTTIE

Dottie and Karen of Penrith Mountain Rescue Team had attended all sorts of search and rescue missions, from train crashes to fallen climbers, but they had yet to make that crucial first find...

Karen Frith, a member of Penrith Mountain Rescue Team, covering the area of the north-east Lake District and northern Pennines, UK, began to train her Border collie puppy, Dottie, to work as a mountain rescue search dog in 2005. By February 2008, when Dottie celebrated her third birthday, she had been fully qualified for just over a year.

One cold evening the emergency pager went off, alerting Karen that her help was needed. Immediately Dottie, who was by now used to the routine of searches and the build-up to them, began to bark and jump up at Karen, as she made her preparations for the search.

> *I quickly grabbed a rucksack, made some sandwiches and a flask of tea and we left the house. All the pager said was 'dogs required in search for missing male', so I drove straight to the rendezvous, the police station. On arrival I met up with four other dog handlers and all the dogs went through the usual rigmarole of greeting each other (which, for the male dogs, mainly involved peeing up the car tyres for several minutes!). We left them outside and went to be briefed by the local police.*

They were told that they were looking for a gentleman who was on medication and required an oxygen supply. He had been missing from a nearby care home since earlier in the day. Dottie and Karen were allocated an area of woodland to search next to a large body of water. The night was rapidly closing in and there was no light other than their torches:

> *We searched in lines through the densely overgrown woods, sometimes wading in water to our knees. It's eerie searching in woodland at night – you just catch a flash of light from the dog jacket and hear the bell jangling in the distance whilst the dog*

> *slips through the undergrowth. Your eyes try*
> *to become accustomed to the lack of light*
> *and you imagine all sorts of noises. The only*
> *consistent and comforting thing is your little*
> *collie, who will occasionally return to you*
> *and slip her nose into your hand as if to*
> *reassure you.*

That night the search was unsuccessful, and after about four intense hours the team stood down. The dogs were given the reward of a quick ball game before everyone went home for some rest before an early start the following morning.

After discussing the search with the police, it was decided that Dottie and Karen would concentrate on an area of woodland close to where they had searched the previous night. They began working through the woods, using a set compass bearing as their guide. After a few minutes, Dottie began to work further away; Karen couldn't see her but could hear the regular sound of her bell marking out her location.

> *Suddenly I saw Dottie appear, running*
> *towards me with her tongue lolling and*
> *her tail wagging madly. She got within a*
> *couple of metres of me and barked loudly*
> *in excitement. Well, this is what we trained*
> *for, I thought – but was it real? Had she*
> *found the man we were searching for? I*
> *gave her the command to take me back to*
> *the casualty ('Show me!') and she ran back*
> *into the woods, zigzagging through the*

trees. When I caught up with her she was barking hysterically at some fallen wood. My heart sank – clearly she was just playing. Yet she wouldn't stop barking; she became so insistent that she ran to me and nipped at my trouser leg. I bent down and there, tucked right under a fallen tree, was our missing man. He was blue and extremely cold – barely alive, in fact. My little dog stopped barking and cuddled in close to the casualty as if to try and help me warm him.

After the initial shock of finding the man and dealing with the immediate first aid, Karen called for assistance from the other searchers. Soon they had him stabilised and on a stretcher, and carried him to a waiting ambulance. Dottie would not leave the man until he was handed over to the paramedics and was certain that he was safe. The man had a great deal to be grateful to Dottie for – had it not been for the tenacity of the little black and white collie, the man could easily have died of exposure.

Karen had nothing but praise for little Dottie: 'My pride in my dog is immense; the loyalty, commitment and perseverance she shows when on searches – in all weathers, any condition and even late at night – is amazing. She does it for me but she also does it because she loves it. I will always be in awe of her.'

BRIAR

*Search and rescue dog Briar was off duty and enjoying
a walk with her handler, Neil Hamilton Bulger, when
the pair made an unexpected discovery...*

It was May 2007 and Neil Hamilton had been walking Briar,
a trained search dog, on the fells close to High Corrie on the
Isle of Arran in Scotland. On returning from the summit of
the fell, Neil decided to take a shortcut and headed north
along a forestry fence. After ten minutes or so, Briar ran off
in the opposite direction to Neil, a few hundred metres along
the path from where they had just come. Some minutes went
by and Briar came bounding back towards Neil.

> *I thought this was very strange, as she always
> likes to keep me in sight, apart from when
> she is working. She started indicating to me,
> as she would when she is working and has
> found a person. When we are out walking
> she picks up people's scent quite often, but
> she just stands rigid with her nose in the
> air for a few seconds and then continues
> on. When we work the dogs we put them
> in jackets or specially designed harnesses; it
> puts them into a frame of mind that would
> best be described as 'working mode'.*

The difference between 'working mode' and just a normal
walk is an important distinction for working dogs; for

example, when a helicopter flies over Neil's house, Briar is often known to run and hide under the bed, but when she has her working jacket on she is eager to be the first to climb into the helicopter to be taken to the search site. On this day, Briar was behaving as though she was on a search and rescue mission, even though she wasn't wearing her jacket.

> *To start with I thought Briar was mucking about and told her to stop being silly and tried to get her to walk on. But she wouldn't have it; she was barking and jumping up, and when I tried to move away she wouldn't let me. So, I thought I would just play along and I told her to show me what she had found.*

As soon as Neil had given this instruction, Briar raced back off in the direction she had come from. Neil followed her down into a gully, to a stream called the Corrie Burn.

> *When I arrived there was Briar, standing next to a man, who was sitting in a heap next to the burn. He was in quite a bad way – his face was covered in blood and he was very dazed. From what I could get from him he had gone for a drink from the burn and fallen in face first. He had taken the impact to his hands and face.*

After Neil cleaned him up with dressings from his first-aid kit the man wanted to make his way back to the path. They walked down the fell and found a seat near to a track. While Neil was phoning for an ambulance, the man's wife appeared on the track with her car and took him to hospital herself. The 57-year-old walker later discharged himself from hospital after treatment for a broken nose and facial lacerations.

> *I don't know why Briar decided to take it on herself to find the man and let me know. Maybe she smelt the blood or a certain scent that she recognised as fear, I just don't know. A few weeks later a 'thank you' letter arrived at our business, addressed to Briar, with a bank note to buy her a squeaky toy (her usual reward for finding someone).*

Briar has since been involved in the detection of two more people whilst on duty for the Arran Mountain Rescue Team.

BARRY

Barry lived from 1800 to 1814 and was a mountain rescue dog living with the monks at the monastery of St Bernard Pass near the Swiss–Italian border...

The St Bernard Pass sits at just over 8,000 feet above sea level in the western Alps. The 49-mile path through the pass is only free from snow for a short period during the summer and it has always proved a treacherous route. Around AD 1050, an Augustine monk named St Bernard de Menthon founded a hospice and monastery in the pass and the monks later began to run rescue missions to save stranded trekkers after snowstorms.

At the start of the eighteenth century, servants were sent out to accompany travellers between the hospice and Bourg-Saint-Pierre on the Swiss side of the pass. By 1750, the servants were usually accompanied by dogs of what later came to be known as the St Bernard breed, which would walk in front of the travellers, clearing a path through the snow with their broad chests. These dogs had a highly attuned sense of direction and were well adapted to withstanding the extreme cold weather. Their acute sense of smell meant they were able to locate people buried deep in the snow.

The monks began to send them out in packs of two or three to search for lost or injured travellers. When they found someone injured buried in the snow, one dog would dig through the snow and lie on top of them to provide warmth, while another dog would return to the hospice to raise the alarm. Popular legend has it that the dogs carried casks of liquor strapped to their collars to revive freezing travellers, but there are no historical records of this practice. Over the course of nearly 200 years, the canines helped in the rescue of around 2,000 people, from lost children to Napoleon's soldiers.

One name stands out amongst these dogs: Barry, who is recorded as assisting in 40 rescues. His most famous and often cited rescue was that of a young boy who was stranded on an icy ledge. The story goes that Barry was sent down the precipice to the boy because none of the men in the rescue team could reach him. The boy was unconscious and covered in thick snow, which was still falling. Barry is said to have inched his way along the ledge towards the frozen boy, then started licking the child's face. After a time the boy was woken by Barry's warm licks and wrapped his arms around the dog's neck, allowing the strong dog to pull him up from the ledge and to safety.

When Barry died his body was preserved, and it is still on display today at the Natural History Museum in Bern, Switzerland. A monument to him was erected at the entrance to the Cimetière des Chiens pet cemetery in Paris.

ST BERNARDS: A BREED WITH A HISTORY

The monks at Great St Bernard Hospice first acquired their famous dogs to serve as companions and watchdogs sometime in the 1660s. They were descendants of the mastiff-style Asiatic dogs brought over by the Romans. This breed was smaller in size than the St Bernards we know today, and had shorter reddish-brown and white fur and a longer tail.

The breed living at the hospice was nearly wiped out between 1816 and 1818, when many dogs died in avalanches during particularly severe weather. In 1830, the monks began to experiment with cross-breeding the dogs with Newfoundlands, in the hope that the longer hair of this breed would help to protect them from the cold, but they soon discovered that ice would form on the longer hairs, making the dogs less effective in their rescues.

In 1855, innkeeper Heinrich Schumacher set up a breeding programme. He supplied the hospice with dogs and also exported them to England, Russia and the USA. The exported dogs were often bred indiscriminately with breeds such as English mastiffs. In 1880, the Swiss Kennel Club officially gave the breed of dogs raised at the hospice the name St Bernard.

In 2004, the Barry Foundation was formed and kennels were established in Martigny, a village near to the pass. On average, 20 St Bernard puppies are born there every year.

KENO

Keno, a five-year-old Labrador retriever from British Columbia, helped make a dramatic rescue after an avalanche...

Ryan Radchenko, a ski lift operator at Fernie Alpine Resort in British Columbia, USA was skiing off-piste on the day before the resort opened to the public for the season when tonnes of snow broke loose from a ridge and tumbled down on top of him in the Currie Bowl, one of the resort's best areas for the powder snow loved by skiers. The area where Ryan was buried was fairly small, but that still didn't leave the rescue team much time.

Robin Siggers, who was head of the Fernie Alpine Resort mountain rescue team and was in charge of four canine rescue dogs, including Keno, at the time of the accident, explained the chances of surviving being buried in an avalanche.

> *Statistically they say you have about a fifty per cent chance after thirty minutes. Less than four per cent of people ever survive being buried more than two metres deep. Once you're six feet down, you're as good as gone because it's going to take half an hour to dig you up.*

Within two minutes of being dispatched onto the scene, Keno had found Ryan's glove, allowing the team to locate Ryan and dig him out. He was unconscious and buried under one metre of snow with his hand reaching above him – he had been trapped for just 26 minutes.

Ryan was rushed to hospital, but was back on site after an hour, safe, sound and well, to the huge relief of Siggers and the rest of the staff. A wooden plaque from the Canadian Avalanche Rescue Dogs Association was hung above Siggers' desk. It read: 'First Live Find. Congratulations Keno and Robin.'

BORIS

Boris the Staffie's sad life on the streets was set to change dramatically and quickly from the day he was rescued...

A neglected Staffordshire bull terrier who had a terrible skin condition when he was rescued by the RSPCA in March

2016 quickly proved that he had it in him to become a top drugs dog for the police.

Boris was the fifth rescue Staffie from the RSPCA's West Hatch animal centre in Taunton, Somerset, UK to join the police force, going from a stray who loved to fetch a tennis ball to a fully licensed police sniffer dog for Avon and Somerset Police in a matter of months.

Sue Dicks, supervisor at West Hatch, said: 'I just knew the minute I saw Boris that he was going to stand out from the crowd. The trainer at the police force, PC Lee Webb, was in the centre the day Boris arrived and I jokingly pointed out that we may have just taken on his next search dog – I couldn't have been more spot on. I noticed quite quickly that he had a real love for tennis balls, he absolutely lives for them. Most dogs get bored after a while, but Boris was really focused – he found the ball when I hid it, even in some rather difficult places like up trees. That was when I knew for sure he would make a great police search dog.'

PC Webb trained Boris to sniff out drugs, firearms and currency. He said:

> Good police dogs need to have an above average ability to retrieve, great stamina, good health and an even temperament. This is why Staffies work so well as they have a dogged determination and a drive to retrieve but are also very loyal and eager to please. Boris is a great dog who has worked really hard and I know he will have a great career ahead of him.

CHAPTER 4

HELPING HUMANS UNDER ANIMAL ATTACK

Whether it's a tiny dachshund tackling a giant bear or a loyal husky taking a rattlesnake bite in place of his owner, there is something deeply touching about a dog putting its own life at risk in an effort to prevent a person coming to harm at the claws of a wild creature.

Relative size and potential danger don't seem to come into it when a dog takes on another creature posing a threat to humans – and, as this selection of stories shows, nor does the question of whether those humans are the dog's loved ones or complete strangers. The acts of bravery documented here are astounding, utterly selfless, and usually completely unbidden, with these super dogs acting entirely on their own initiative and instincts.

DAISY

A tiny dachshund showed no fear when a gigantic bear threatened to attack her beloved humans, putting her own life on the line rather than see any harm come to them…

When Daisy the miniature dachshund heard Krystal Long scream outside their house in Florida, USA she instinctively ran out of the open front door, along with Krystal's six-year-old son, to do what she could to protect her beloved owner. That was when the seven-kilogram sausage dog found herself up against a mighty 90-kilogram bear that had wandered into the garage, attracted by the smell of the groceries that Krystal was unloading from the car.

On seeing the bear in her garage, Krystal said: 'I really thought that I was going to die and I wasn't sure what was going to happen to my son. I started throwing things at it to get it to go away because usually when you do that, they take off. But this bear was different. It only enraged him and made him come closer.'

Daisy, however, was undeterred, and hurled herself at the bear, distracting the huge animal long enough for Krystal to bundle her young son safely back inside the house. When she came back out, to her horror she saw that the bear had pinned down the little dog and was ripping into her. Grabbing the nearest heavy object – a gas canister – she threw it at the bear, startling it enough that it turned and ran, allowing Daisy to nip under the car to safety.

In distracting the bear, the courageous little canine had possibly saved two lives – but she had also sustained severe injuries, including lacerations and broken ribs that required expensive surgery – money that the family didn't have. Before long, however, money started rolling in from well-wishers – more than enough to cover the thousands of dollars needed to put daring Daisy on the road to a full recovery!

TESS

Fay Palethorpe and her kelpie, Tess, had a close call one Sunday morning when they came across a deadly eastern brown snake in their garden...

Retiree Fay Palethorpe, aged 68 at the time, was in the garden of her Tallebudgera Valley home on Australia's Gold Coast with her one-year-old kelpie pup, Tess, and her two other kelpies, when she spotted a snake lying on a rock. At about 1.8 metres in length, it was the biggest she had ever seen. It reared up the instant it saw Fay and lunged at her. As Fay screamed out and turned to run, the three dogs darted in front of her and began attacking the snake.

Fay's immediate response was to call the dogs off – from its brown scales she guessed the snake might be a poisonous eastern brown, and knew that a bite to one of her pets could be fatal. Two of them obeyed her command, but the youngest, Tess, continued her attack on the reptile, throwing it back and forth through the air. Then there was a sudden yelp – Tess had been bitten on the ear.

The injured snake managed to slither away in the confusion that followed, but now Fay's attention was focused on getting her brave dog to the vet in time to save her. As it was a Sunday morning she had to ring around for an emergency vet, and Tess was in a bad way by the time they reached the surgery in Tugun. She was administered antivenom and put on an intravenous drip to try to flush the rest of the poison out.

Fay lives alone on her 20-acre property, so had she been bitten, it could have been too late by the time she was able to receive treatment. The eastern brown snake has fast-acting venom and is the second most venomous land snake in the world; though around half of patients respond well to the antivenom, about 50 per cent do not recover. Fay had to borrow money from her son in order to pay the emergency treatment bill, even though there was no guarantee that Tess would recover – but it was worth it for the dog that had saved her life. Happily, within a week of being bitten, Tess came out of the coma she had slipped into and made a full recovery.

DID YOU KNOW? DOGS CAN BE TRAINED TO AVOID RATTLESNAKES

A bite from a rattlesnake can be deadly within minutes, and even when a dog survives a bite, its neurological system will be permanently affected. A rattlesnake vaccine is available, but in southern US states such as Arizona, Georgia, Florida, Alabama, South Carolina and Texas, where temperatures in the spring reach levels that encourage the snakes to come out of hibernation, snake-avoidance training is often carried out on high-risk dogs.

The aversion training involves giving a dog a quick electric shock from a special collar (the strength of the shock is geared to the size of the dog) every time it approaches the training snake, that has had either its fangs or its venom removed. Usually it takes a maximum of three shocks to stop the dog ever going near a snake again, as it rapidly comes to associate the pain of the shock with the sight of the snake.

But it is a rattlesnake's distinctive smell that is the first thing a dog senses when it is in the proximity of one – before seeing it or hearing the rattle – and some avoidance trainers base their technique on the fact that with its highly sensitive nose, a dog can smell a snake 50 metres away. This enables them to train even blind dogs to stay away from the lethal reptiles.

SHADOW

Most of us were afraid of the 'big bad wolf' in fairy tales when we were little, but few parents nowadays are confronted with the horror of a pair of hungry wolves closing in on their children...

On 22 December, the Keays family and their friend Rod Barrie were on a pre-Christmas tobogganing outing about sixty miles from Fort Nelson, Canada. It was 3.30 p.m. and darkness was beginning to fall when Shadow, the Keays' Rottweiler cross and family pet, suddenly wrenched his lead out of the hands of Mrs Keays and bounded across the snow in the direction of one of the sleighs, aboard which sat her three young children. She let out a scream of terror when she saw the reason for Shadow's determined running: two wolves had appeared from nowhere and were fast closing in on the sleigh.

Kyle Keays, the children's father, who was riding an ATV (quad bike) some distance away, saw Shadow intercept the lead wolf. It hit Shadow in the shoulder, who quickly spun round and grabbed it by the face. Keays was too far away to help and so hurried off towards his work camp nearby to get a rifle. Rod Barrie, who was towing the children in the sleigh when the wolves approached, managed to remain calm and continue towards his truck, which was parked not far away with his wife sitting inside.

When he reached the truck, the wolves were just six metres away, but he and his wife managed to pull the terrified children into the safety of the truck just in time. Armed with a shovel, Barrie began swiping at the wolves to keep them at bay.

By now Barrie had been able to take a good look at the wolves and could see their bones were protruding: they must have been starving. Shadow continued to growl at them, but they stood their ground, until Barrie jumped on his ATV and succeeded in driving them away some 20 metres, allowing them to get Shadow inside the truck and drive away.

Back at the Keays' work camp they examined Shadow – he'd been lucky enough to escape with minor cuts and bruises. But the hungry wolves hadn't given up; a short while later the lead wolf appeared at the camp. Keays, a licensed hunter, was able to track the wolf and shoot her. He later found and shot the second wolf.

It is highly unusual for wolves to prey on humans, and in all his years of hunting Keays said he'd never had such a close encounter with these elusive animals. Luckily, Shadow was with them when the surprise attack happened, and his protective instincts prompted him to save the day.

HAUS

A young German shepherd rescue dog was willing to sacrifice himself to protect a little girl he adored...

A rescue dog repaid the family who adopted him from a rescue centre in Florida, USA by saving their seven-year-old daughter Molly from a potentially lethal snakebite – suffering three dangerous bites himself in the process.

Adam DeLuca, Molly's father, hadn't initially wanted any dog to replace their previous family dog who had died at 13 years old. But Donya, his wife, was determined to provide two-year-old Haus with a new home, and he quickly won over everybody's hearts.

She said: 'He just bonded with all of us so quickly, it was like he was always part of our home. Even the neighbours took to him. It was meant to be. Especially at night, he's very protective of the kids. He follows them around, he takes care of them.'

The German shepherd's love of the two young children, Molly and Joey, nearly cost him his life when he was bitten in May 2016. 'He instantly positioned himself between the snake and Molly, so at first, she and her grandma didn't even realize what he was staring at – but then all of a sudden there was all of this blood,' said Donya.

He needed to be put on a constant drip of antivenom as the eastern diamondback rattlesnake, the snake that is thought to have bitten him on his front leg, is one of the most dangerous venomous snakes in North America. Although there had been the possibility of kidney damage, miraculously Haus was expected to make a full recovery.

The treatment was very costly though, but donations immediately came flooding in from all over the world, reaching more than double the $28,000 the family needed to pay the emergency vet's bill. They planned to donate the rest to the rescue centre where Haus had come from and to other local animal shelters. 'People always want to adopt a puppy, because it's a puppy,' she said. 'But adult dogs need homes too, and I hope my story will encourage people to go find their own Haus, who's just as deserving of a home as a puppy,' said Donya.

Haus made a full recovery and received the 'Heroic Dog Award' from PETA (People for the Ethical Treatment of Animals) for his bravery – as well as a much-deserved bag of doggie treats!

ANGEL

*A golden retriever started acting out of
character, but her young owner didn't realise
why until it was almost too late...*

When his pet dog Angel started acting strangely around him one day, sticking closer to him than she usually did, 11-year-old Austin Forman of Boston Bar, British Columbia in Canada didn't think anything more about it. But he wished he had when, while he was gathering firewood in the back yard of his family home, a cougar suddenly appeared from nowhere and charged at him. He realised in that awful moment that Angel must have had some sort of premonition about the attack, or at least some awareness of the cougar's presence in the area, and had been trying to protect him.

And protect him she did! The golden retriever leapt at the wild cat to prevent it from attacking Austin, and fought it while the boy ran into the house to alert his mother, Sherri.

Sherri immediately called the police, who responded quickly and killed the cougar – but not before it had inflicted serious injuries on the brave dog.

Angel was taken to the Sardis Animal Hospital, where she was treated for deep bites and scratches and thankfully recovered completely – to be rewarded for her bravery with a large steak, bought for her by young Austin, whose life she had saved.

BERRY

When Julie Closuit took her dog Berry out for her usual toilet break, she wasn't expecting a dramatic confrontation with a grumpy moose...

Every morning, before Julie would take her Rottweiler Berry out to go to the toilet, she would first check for the neighbour's dog or for any stray moose in the vicinity of her home in Fairbanks, Alaska, USA (during the winter, when they're hungry and their energy levels are low, moose can become aggressive and are less likely to retreat if they see a human). This morning was no different, and after shining her torch around the corner of the house in the dark, Julie, six months pregnant at the time, decided it was safe to bring the dog out.

A short while later, three-year-old Berry began barking frantically. Julie assumed it must be the neighbour's dog, but as she shone her torch in the direction the dog was barking, she glimpsed the silhouette of a moose behind a spruce tree about six metres away. She saw its ears go back and it began to charge towards them.

Before she had a chance to decide what to do, Berry yanked the leash out of her hand and rushed off towards the moose, circling behind it in a C-shaped herding pattern.

Julie followed the advice her parents had always given her in the event of such a situation – she dived behind some birch trees for protection, just in time to see the moose run past where she had been standing.

Berry rejoined Julie as she pulled herself up, just as the moose began its second charge. But Berry put herself between her owner and the moose, barking ferociously until the moose began to retreat back towards the house. As it did so, Berry ran over and headed it off, forcing it to turn back in the direction of the woods. Berry continued to bark until she seemed sure that the moose wasn't coming back.

Rottweilers are most commonly used as guard dogs, but originally they were bred for herding animals – perhaps this explains Berry's response and fast action. Though the whole incident probably only lasted 30 seconds, it made a lasting impression on Julie, who subsequently erected a fence around her property in the hope of preventing future altercations with the local moose population.

DOBERMANN VS. DEADLY COBRA

The owner of a Dobermann pinscher was away from home when he received a surprise phone call from his neighbour, who told him to turn on the news and watch a clip of his brave dog defending the family property from a deadly cobra...

When Puzhandi's pet Dobermann pinscher spotted a 2.1-metre-long cobra trying to sneak into his owner's home in Chennai, India, a fierce battle on the lawn ensued, attracting a small crowd of onlookers from the neighbourhood. The crowd watched, enthralled, as the cobra, hood raised and hissing, dodged in between plants. The dog skilfully darted about just out of reach, before finally moving in for the attack and grasping the snake between its teeth, smashing it against the ground until it died. The fearless dog subsequently became somewhat of a local celebrity – the battle had been filmed and broadcast on news channels.

It was unfortunate that the cobra had to die rather than being humanely removed: cobras feed almost entirely on other snakes and only attack humans if provoked or in a situation where they are trapped and feel threatened. However, had the snake entered the property it could have posed a danger to the unsuspecting family when they returned home. Dobermanns are for the most part a gentle, loyal and highly intelligent breed, but they will attack in response to a perceived threat to themselves, their territory or family.

TUMBLEWEED

*A loyal dog took a potentially lethal
snakebite to save his owner...*

When Tumbleweed the husky cross came bowling over towards his owner David Crowell, who was outside his house in Hesperia, California, USA picking plums, David didn't think anything of it until the dog suddenly leapt back as he got near. At that point David spotted a rattlesnake at his feet, and realised that the dog – his best friend – had been trying to protect him from the venomous creature.

But what he didn't realise for another hour was that, in defending him from the snake, Tumbleweed had taken a bite on his nose, that now started to swell up.

Luckily, David managed to rush his brave dog to the local animal medical centre in time, where a number of dogs had already been treated for rattlesnake bites that year. There, Tumbleweed was given antivenom, antibiotics and an antihistamine and was later allowed to go home, having made a full recovery.

As for the bond between man and dog, it got that much stronger as a result of the incident.

David said: '[Tumbleweed] is my hero, because he definitely saved me. If it wasn't for him I might have been the one that was bitten.'

CHAPTER 5

HELPING OTHER ANIMALS IN DISTRESS

What drives a dog to plunge into a lake to rescue a bag full of tiny stray kittens, to see off a wild coyote threatening the neighbour's chihuahua, or to suckle a young and desperately needy abandoned kitten? Why dogs seem so ready to risk their own lives or to be willing to deviate from the norm to save another creature is a mystery and will likely remain one. But such selflessness is one of the many reasons they pull on our heartstrings and command such love and devotion from their respective humans.

The stories in this chapter highlight dogs' capacity to be instinctively aware of the distress of other living creatures and to treat such creatures with the gentle care and compassion that we might assume they would reserve purely for their own offspring.

HAPPY

A gentle giant of a Rottweiler foiled a coyote's plans for breakfast in the form of the tiny chihuahua cross next door!

When Happy the Rottweiler suddenly heard a frightened squeal early one morning, he glanced across his yard and saw a coyote – previously unheard of in that built-up neighbourhood – with its jaws clamped around the black chihuahua-dachshund cross ('Chiweenie') next door, trying to make off with her.

Little Trixxie had been chained up outside just after breakfast while her owners got ready in the house, and the opportunist coyote clearly saw her as its next meal. The tiny dog tried to run back inside, but the coyote quickly outran her and grabbed her in its mouth. Because she was attached to the chain, it couldn't carry her away, but it had her in its jaws for around ten seconds.

That was when Trixxie squealed – and when Happy leapt to her rescue, hurtling across the two yards and startling the coyote into dropping her. He then chased the wild animal off while the little dog scampered to safety.

Trixxie's shaken owners later watched the whole episode unfold, as it was captured on a security camera outside their property. As for the little Chiweenie, she suffered only minor puncture wounds, and was far less bothered by the incident than her humans, who vowed never to leave her chained up outside again.

And Happy proved once and for all that Rottweilers, despite their unfortunate reputation for being vicious, can be as gentle, loyal and heroic as the next dog when their next-door neighbour is fighting for her life!

HARLEY

A tiny maimed dog rescued from a caged existence showed he had a huge heart and a willingness to bring the horrors of puppy farming to the attention of the world...

Whether they're called puppy mills or puppy farms, the horrendous conditions in which dogs used purely for breeding and their young ones are kept are the same, as are the physical and mental scars that the animals kept in these appalling conditions are left with.

Harley, a tiny brindle chihuahua, was rescued from one such place in America after spending ten years in a cage and nearly being thrown away like rubbish when he was no longer of any use. With a diseased heart, a rot-eaten mouth, a fused spine, a broken tail, gnarled toes and deformed legs – as well as a missing eye due to his cage being power-washed while he was still in it – he has become a willing and devoted spokesdog against puppy mills.

The brave little dog makes public appearances all over the USA, at schools and events where, while acting as a very powerful statement about the horrors of puppy mills and puppy farms, he enjoys plenty of love and attention – things that were sorely missing in his incarcerated former life.

His own journey to freedom and better health has resulted in a fundraising campaign called 'Harley to the Rescue', that has saved and provided funds for the medical treatment of over 500 dogs rescued from similar establishments. He even goes on the rescue missions himself, looking after the terrified dogs as they are released from the nightmarish conditions.

Grizzled little Harley won the 2015 Emerging Hero Award from the American Humane Association, giving further strength to his mission to help the many thousands of breeding bitches, stud dogs and litters of puppies still suffering in puppy mills and puppy farms the world over.

PUPPY FARMS

Puppy farms are establishments where dogs are bred in cages in high numbers, with little or no regard for the health and welfare of the puppies or their parents.

A puppy farmer's main goal is profit. As a result, they typically focus on 'designer' breeds that are in high demand and fetch a lot of money, getting as many litters as they possibly can from each breeding bitch (even though the Kennel Club will not normally register more than four litters from any one bitch), and separating puppies from their mothers too early.

The puppies are rarely socialised and often suffer from common, preventable, infectious diseases and painful or chronic inherited conditions. They frequently have more behavioural issues and shorter life spans than those bred in more humane conditions. Those that aren't sold are killed inhumanely to save costs, or are kept on to suffer the same fate as their parents, becoming perpetual breeding dogs.

There are several anti-puppy-farm campaigns in the UK, including C.A.R.I.A.D. and Four Paws, as well as many equivalent organisations opposed to puppy mills in the USA.

The Kennel Club is trying to persuade the government to update legislation aimed at lessening the demand for puppy farm puppies, as well as educating the public about puppy farms and improving breeding standards.

As a result of irresponsible breeding practices and a lack of neutering programmes in many countries, there are thousands and thousands of unwanted and desperate dogs all over the world – so why not give one of them a forever home instead?

DID YOU KNOW?

If never spayed or neutered, a female dog, her mate, and their puppies could produce over 66,000 dogs in six years!

CHLOE

*A dog and cat's fondness for each other was firmly
sealed when the cat fell into an icy pond...*

A little pug called Chloe proved her devotion to her
best friend Willow, a Siamese cat, by raising the alarm
when she fell into a freezing pond at their home in
Montana, USA.

With an unusually strong bond, Chloe and Willow had
always done everything together – including both walking
with their humans, Amanda and Ron Bjelland, to pick up the
daily newspaper from the front yard where it was dropped
by the delivery boy.

But one particular day back in March 2010, while Chloe
went back into the house with them after collecting the
newspaper, Willow carried on round to the back yard – and
that was where she got into trouble, falling into the ice-
covered fish pond.

Suddenly, Chloe started frantically barking and scratching
at the back door, and when Ron let her out, she carried on
crying in a very distressed way. So, puzzled by the dog's
strange behaviour, Ron followed her out, to find Willow
struggling to get out of the pond. He thought that by the
time he pulled her out she must have been in the icy water
for around 20 minutes.

The shivering cat, who had certainly used up one of her
nine lives, made a full recovery once she had warmed up
– and Chloe, her saviour, was rewarded for her life-saving
efforts with a doggie treat.

The unlikely pair have since become even better friends as a result of their watery adventure!

LILO

When a tiny abandoned kitten was struggling to survive, who else to turn to but Lilo, a motherly husky?

Lilo the husky will never have puppies of her own, but her innate motherly instincts have saved the life of a tiny kitten who has grown up to think she's a dog!

Rosie the kitten was rescued as a stray at three weeks old in the spring of 2015 by three Californian sisters – Thi, Tram and Thoa Bui – but rejected food and was so sickly and weak that even with round-the-clock care she nearly didn't survive the night. In a last-ditch effort to keep her alive, the sisters paired her up with Lilo, one of their three Siberian huskies, who immediately took on the role of surrogate mother, allowing little Rosie to suckle on her and, in the way her real mother would have done, stimulating her to toilet.

Thi Bui said:

> Her eyes became infected and closed. We were providing all the human care we could, but we realized she needed a mother so we paired her with Lilo, one of our huskies. Amazingly, Lilo took on the motherhood role instantly, which was surprising because

she has no pups of her own and was spayed
the week before we got the kitten.

The pair rapidly became inseparable, with Rosie content to snuggle into Lilo's soft downy fur and proving herself a quick learner. Among the other skills Lilo has taught her feline charge are walking with a pack of dogs – the sisters have two other huskies, Infinity and Miko – and panting like a husky! The unlikely group eat, sleep and play together, and Rosie likes to sneak dog food whenever she can. The adventurous kitten has even joined the sisters on kayaking and paddle-boarding trips!

Rosie is not the only tiny creature Lilo has saved with her mothering skills – she has acted as surrogate mum to several other rescued animals, and seems to have found her true calling in life. And as for Rosie, more recently she's even copied her canine mum in fostering nine rescued kittens herself!

JASMINE

In 2008, Jasmine the wonder dog adopted a fawn
called Bramble, the fiftieth animal she had become
surrogate mother to by the age of just seven...

Police found Jasmine abandoned in a garden shed and brought her to the Nuneaton and Warwickshire Wildlife Sanctuary in the UK in 2003. The little greyhound was shivering and desperately undernourished, and needed a lot of love and care before she could begin to trust the staff at the sanctuary.

Once Jasmine had made a full recovery, she began to demonstrate a unique talent for caring for other injured animals brought to the sanctuary. Director of the sanctuary Geoff Grewcock explained that greyhounds can be an aggressive breed – which is why they are used for racing – so he was surprised at the amount of affection she displayed for other creatures, particularly as she had been so neglected herself.

Since arriving at the sanctuary, Jasmine had cared for five fox cubs, four badger cubs, 15 chicks, eight guinea pigs, two stray puppies and 15 rabbits. 'She simply dotes on the animals as if they were her own, it's incredible to see,' said Greg. 'She licks the rabbits and guinea pigs and even lets the birds perch on the bridge of her nose.'

Greg recalled one incident when two puppies, a Lakeland terrier cross and a Jack Russell-Dobermann cross, found dumped by a nearby railway line were brought in to the sanctuary. 'They were tiny when they arrived at the centre and Jasmine approached them and grabbed one by the scruff of the neck in her mouth and put him on the settee. Then she fetched the other one and sat down with them, cuddling them.'

Jasmine's fiftieth protégée, Bramble, was an 11-week-old roe deer fawn found semi-conscious in a field by a man who was out walking his dog. Jasmine instantly took the little fawn under her care, cuddling up close to keep her warm, making sure nothing got matted in her fur and showing her lots of love. 'They walk together round the sanctuary,' said Greg. 'It's a real treat to see them.' Jasmine cared for the fawn until she was old enough to be released back into the wild.

SURROGATE MOTHERS

Lilo and Jasmine are not the only canines to have displayed such an overwhelming and non-discerning maternal instinct.

Vasile Borza, a farmer from Hodişel village in Bihor, Romania, was shocked to discover that his pet dog Lola had nursed two piglets that he had left for dead back to health.

And Lisha, a nine-year-old Labrador owned by the director of Cango Wildlife Reserve in the Oudtshoorn area of South Africa, was credited with playing surrogate mother to at least 30 baby animals, including a porcupine, a hippo, two cheetah cubs and three tiger cubs. The animals were either orphans or had been rejected by their natural mothers, proving that dogs aren't just wonderful to humans – they can be superheroes to all creatures!

REX

Leonie was surprised one afternoon when her dog Rex brought home an unusual present for her...

Leonie Allan was out walking her ten-year-old pointer cross Rex one morning when she saw a dead kangaroo at the side of the road near her home. Roadkill was not an uncommon sight where she lives in Victoria, Australia, so she thought nothing more of it until later that day.

That afternoon Leonie was busy working in her front garden when Rex took up the 'pointing' stance typical of his breed, which indicates that the dog has found something. When he ran off, Leonie was at first worried that he had found a snake, but he then returned to her and dropped a live joey at her feet.

Incredibly, the joey had survived the road accident that had killed its mother. Rex had somehow sensed that the joey was still alive in the dead mother's pouch, and had brought it back so gently that it was unharmed and calm. In fact, Leonie noted that the pair already seemed to be good friends as she watched the joey jump up at Rex and the gentle dog lick the little creature in return. 'I was so surprised and delighted. Rex saved the day,' she said.

The joey was named Rex Jr and was taken to Jirrahlinga Wildlife Sanctuary where he was cared for until he was 18 months old, then released into the wild. The director of the sanctuary, Tehree Gordon, commented on the remarkable nature of the rescue; not only that Rex acted so calmly and gently, but also that the joey didn't see him as a predator and was completely relaxed – she had seen many humans bring joeys into the sanctuary who had accidentally injured the little animals when they struggled and tried to break free. She said: 'It's a lesson that dogs can be raised to be familiar and compatible with wildlife, you just have to teach them right from wrong.'

NAPOLEON

*Alexandra didn't know what had got into
her dog Napoleon – who wasn't a swimmer
– when he dived into a lake...*

Alexandra Breuer from Michigan, USA was out in her garden when Napoleon, her two-year-old white English bulldog, dashed off and leapt into the lake across the road. Bulldogs are not very strong swimmers, and Alexandra wondered what had given Napoleon the sudden notion to take a dip.

Next she saw the dog dragging a bag, which she assumed to be full of rubbish, out of the water and towards the house. But then Alexandra heard muffled meowing, and opened the bag to reveal six kittens. It seemed that Napoleon had heard their little cries for help and ran to their rescue.

Sadly, two of the kittens died, but Alexandra nursed the surviving four back to health and took care of them for two weeks before she could take them along to the local pet adoption centre, where new homes would be found for them.

Napoleon was greeted with applause down at the adoption centre – word had got out about his rescue, and a crowd of fans had gathered to honour the courageous dog whose fast action had saved four little lives.

MILO

Milo didn't have the best start in life. His first owners had abused him, leaving him seriously disabled. But that didn't stop the Westie diving in to the rescue when he spotted another dog in trouble...

When Lynda Pomfret adopted Milo, a six-year-old West Highland terrier, he wasn't in great shape – he had been horribly mistreated by his previous owners and had brain damage and injured legs.

Lynda was out walking Milo along the beach near her home in Appledore, Devon, UK when he saw a spaniel struggling in the water and jumped in to save the animal from drowning. Lynda said of her brave little pooch, 'He's not the sharpest tool in the box but he'll always be a hero to me.'

Milo was later honoured by subscribers to Saga Zone, a social networking site for the over-50s, as winner of the 'PetZfactor 2008' competition. He was voted the most heroic dog out of more than 500 pets that were entered into the competition by their owners.

CHAPTER 6

HELPING PEOPLE

Assistance dogs can vastly improve the quality of life for people with sensory impairments as well as for those with physical and mental health issues. Whether they're helping their human carry out day-to-day functions such as opening doors and collecting money from the ATM for them, or providing companionship to help them through dark days, they're enabling them to carry on with a normal life despite difficulties.

As the stories in this section show, the bond that develops between a person and their assistance dog is incredibly strong, sometimes leading to the dog going above and beyond their duties and acting off their own bat to ensure the safety of their owner.

POPPY

A young epilepsy sufferer got her freedom back thanks to the mysterious powers of her seizure response dog...

Whenever Poppy, a young Labrador, started getting agitated, it was a vital life-saving cue for her owner, Shannon Locke, to prepare herself for an epileptic seizure that, without fail, took place 15 to 20 minutes later.

Scientists have no idea how Poppy knew that Shannon was about to suffer from a dangerous fit – or, once it had taken place, how the remarkable dog knew that she needed to clear Shannon's airways and stop her from choking by licking the saliva away until the episode was over and she was safe again.

But however she did it, her presence by Shannon's side gave the woman from County Down, Northern Ireland, her life back.

Shannon explained:

> *I have seizures a couple of times a week and they can be very serious. They can be fatal. They began when I was about seventeen and they were getting horrendous at one stage, when I was having them four or five times a day. I couldn't leave the house and couldn't work. Then Poppy came along and has been a real lifeline. One day she just started to act strange, I'd no idea why. She just kept coming up to me and was panting. I didn't think much of it to begin with, but then I realised she was picking up that something wasn't right.*

Shannon embarked on a mission to tell the world about her life-saving canine best friend, and made a video showing Poppy in action. By 2016, the film had been viewed several million times and had helped raised awareness of the amazing powers of so-called seizure response dogs, which can be trained to assist in a variety of ways. Some are trained to bark when a person has a seizure to alert others to the emergency, while others lie next to the person having the fit to prevent injury, and some can be trained to activate alarms.

Poppy's own incredible abilities were examined by experts at Queen's University Belfast as part of a study to determine how dogs can be used to help epilepsy sufferers around the world.

HOW DO DOGS DETECT SEIZURES?

Some scientists have suggested that the electrical activity that leads to a seizure begins in the brain up to an hour and a half before the patient demonstrates any outward signs. This activity is thought to take place in the part of the brain that regulates heartbeat and perspiration. With their acute sense of smell, dogs would be able to detect these changes.

ENDAL

Barking for attention at the local pub and handing over money for beer may not be an assistance dog's most important duty, but it was just one of the many things that put a one-in-a-million Labrador at the centre of his disabled owner's life...

During his 12 years of life, Endal the Labrador saved Allen Parton's life and marriage – a true wonder dog whose memory has been preserved in a book written by Allen, simply called *Endal*, that has since been made into a film.

Allen, from Clanfield in Hampshire, UK ended up in a wheelchair as a result of a car crash while he was serving in the Royal Navy during the Gulf War in 1991. His injuries also affected his memory, and he could no longer recognise his wife and children, leaving him depressed and suicidal.

Enter Endal, who was in the process of being trained by Canine Partners for Independence, the charity for whom Allen's wife worked. The day Allen decided to accompany her to the dog-training centre was the day his life changed forever, as Endal took an instant liking to him, leaping onto his lap and giving him a big doggy kiss.

'It was a cathartic experience which finally gave me the hope I needed,' Allen said. 'Until I met him, I was in the depths of despair. But when he refused to leave my side at the training centre, I suddenly saw a chink of light.'

The pair quickly became inseparable companions, Endal helping Allen with all sorts of everyday tasks, from getting cash out of a cashpoint, picking up the phone and posting letters to pulling his clothes out of the washing machine and gathering his cutlery for lunch. He even saved Allen's life when his wheelchair was knocked over by a car, shoving him into the recovery position, dragging a blanket over him and running to a nearby hotel where he barked for help. Endal was voted Dog of the Millennium for the rescue, for which he was also given the PDSA's prestigious Gold Medal.

The loving Labrador's presence in Allen's life also brought him and his wife back together again after their marriage foundered, and in 2002 they renewed their wedding vows.

But inevitably old age took its toll on Endal, who became crippled with arthritis, and in 2009 he sadly had a stroke, leaving Allen to make the toughest decision of his life.

'I'm afraid I'm not coping with it particularly well. But I couldn't bear to see Endal suffer,' he said later. 'When I finally arrive at the pearly gates myself, I know in my heart of hearts that Endal will be there waiting faithfully for me with his otter-like tail in full swing.'

HOUNDS FOR HEROES

There's an army of wonder dogs helping heroes of the human variety – injured and disabled former members of the UK Armed Forces and Emergency Services

Hounds for Heroes was founded in 2009 and registered in 2010 by the disabled man whom Endal the Labrador assisted, Allen Parton, with the aim of raising the £100,000 needed to provide five assistance dogs. These dogs – all Labradors – were trained to enhance the quality of life of their disabled owners by helping them with daily tasks that they could no longer manage themselves – even opening train doors for them – as well as being loyal companions and bringing them the love that had all too often sadly gone from their lives.

The initial campaign was such a success that by 2016 a fourth campaign was under way to raise funds to support the numerous 'squadrons' of canine recruits either in basic training with volunteer 'puppy parents' or in advanced training at the training base in Petersfield, Hampshire, UK.

These wonder dogs don't just open physical doors for their heroic humans – they often open the door to a new life for them.

MUGLY

*The world's ugliest dog was the most beautiful
on the inside, as well as the most heroic and
selfless when it came to helping others...*

Mugly may have been crowned Britain's Ugliest Dog in 2005, and then have topped it seven years later with the World's Ugliest Dog title, but he didn't let those dubious honours hold him back from helping others and going on to be crowned 'Most Heroic Hound'!

The Chinese Crested dog deservedly scooped the heroic title at the annual SuperDogs awards in 2016, four years after being awarded top-dog honours for his challenging looks. He was named Most Heroic Hound thanks to his tireless work as a certified Pets As Therapy (PAT) Dog as well as for his visits to schools as part of the 'Read to Dogs' scheme where he encourages shy children to read out loud to him to boost their confidence.

Mugly's good deeds seem to be endless. In addition to helping nervous children overcome their fear of dogs and coaxing a deaf-blind man out of his shell, he also takes part in many fundraising events, including those run by Cinque Ports Rescue, Guide Dogs for the Blind, the Chinese Crested Club of GB Rescue and Many Tears Animal Rescue.

His owner Bev Nicholson said:

> *Mugly is a sweet, calm and sensitive dog
> who instantly knows how to behave in
> various situations. He amazes me with his*

ability to know exactly how to be when he meets people. With a blind person he stands completely still and lets them explore him, or when someone is upset he pushes his body into them for comfort. I could just burst with pride when a child bumps into us with their parents who are saying 'don't touch the dog' and the child replies 'oh that's OK, that's Mugly, he won't hurt me, he helps me to read'.

TOBY

A golden retriever saved his owner's life by performing his version of the Heimlich manoeuvre on her...

When Angela Parkhurst of Maryland, USA, choked on a piece of apple that got lodged in her throat, her own efforts to remove it by pounding on her chest failed.

That was when Angela's pet dog Toby heroically stepped in, leaping up to put his paws on her shoulders and push her to the ground, and then jumping up and down on her chest until the apple came out. The two-year-old golden retriever didn't stop there, but carried on with his doggie first aid by licking her face so that she wouldn't pass out.

She ended up with chest and stomach wounds – but with her life too.

Angela, who went on numerous chat shows with Toby to tell their amazing story, said:

I literally have paw-print-shaped bruises on my chest. I'm still a little hoarse, but otherwise I'm OK. They say dogs leave a paw print on your heart. He left a paw print on my heart, that's for sure. The doctor said I probably wouldn't be here without Toby. I keep looking at him and saying, 'You're amazing'.

FLEETWOOD MAC

A disabled chihuahua found his perfect match
in a baby girl born with the same disorder...

It's often said that like attracts like, and that was definitely the case for an eight-year-old unwanted chihuahua suffering from a rare genetic disorder.

No one seemed to want to offer a home to little Fleetwood Mac, who was born with cleft front paws – a congenital deformity called Ectrodactyly, and sometimes known descriptively as 'lobster claw syndrome'.

But then Umbrella of Hope, the animal rescue shelter in San Francisco, USA where he was being looked after, decided to try something that had worked previously with a rescue dog called Fireman who had suffered serious chemical burns. Through their 'perfect match' programme, they had managed to successfully pair Fireman up with a human burns survivor, so now the shelter started looking for someone to adopt Fleetwood who also had Ectrodactyly.

When, as a result of a social media campaign, they came across the Campos family from Indiana, who were looking for a companion pup for the chihuahua they already had, they knew they were on to something, as the Campos's baby daughter Grace had the same syndrome as Fleetwood, having been born with cleft hands and feet.

The 'perfect match' pairing of Fleetwood with Grace was a huge success, and the whole family – as well as Charlie the chihuahua – immediately took to Fleetwood. And not only had the little dog from California found a forever home, the seven-month-old baby girl would grow up with a doggy babysitter and, as she got older, a canine companion who she could relate to and who, with his cleft paws, would help her feel less isolated as a result of her disorder.

LYE

Life took a turn for the worse for Nicola Willis when she lost her hearing, but her canine companion gave her the confidence to enjoy life again and was at her side in times of need...

When Nicola Willis became severely deaf, she became depressed and lost her confidence. She said, 'What really upset me was that I became reliant on other people: I had lost my independence. I stayed in my house, but even that was awful as I just couldn't hear even simple sounds. I was sinking fast.'

She decided to apply for a hearing dog and was delighted when her own 14-month Cavalier King Charles spaniel,

Lye, was assessed by the charity Hearing Dogs for Deaf People and accepted for training. The pair were separated for a difficult four months while Lye was put through her paces at training school, where she learned how to react to various household sounds, including the telephone, doorbell, cooker timer and the 'call' (an instruction other people can give to Lye asking her to fetch Nicola), as well as the danger sounds of the smoke alarm and fire bell. In July 2005 they were reunited, this time with Lye in her smart, burgundy hearing dog working jacket. Since having Lye as a hearing dog, Nicola's life has changed dramatically.

> *When Lye came back to me having been trained, everything changed. Friends started to call on me again, knowing that not only would the front door be opened, but on the other side of the door would be two very happy individuals. It was like the light was shining again. My depression was lifting.*

But Lye's dedication to Nicola didn't stop there. In 2008 Lye acted above and beyond the call of duty on two separate occasions. The first time was on an outing to the shops; Nicola was recovering from a damaged knee at the time and was using crutches.

> *We were taking a shortcut through an alleyway when I fell over, and I just lay on the ground, cold, scared and in pain – I couldn't get up. To my surprise Lye ran off, which upset me even more as she was wearing her hearing dog coat and I thought she might get*

*stolen. After a few minutes I looked up and
saw my beloved dog running back to me with
a man following close behind her. He told me
she had gone to the main street and grabbed
him by the trouser leg. He saw her coat and
realised she must be telling him something so
he followed her. It turned out that he was a
nurse, so Lye picked well!*

Lye's second act of bravery came one night when Nicola
and her daughters were asleep in bed. Nicola had taken
her hearing aids out to go to sleep and was woken by Lye
scrabbling at her chest. At first she thought Lye might need
the toilet so she started to get out of bed, but Lye pulled her
back down and would not let her move. This was very strange
behaviour for Lye, and it was enough to alert Nicola to the
fact that something was wrong. Although her hearing aids do
not fully restore her hearing, as soon as Nicola put them in
she could hear noises she knew must have been coming from
downstairs and realised there were intruders in her house.

*I panicked and didn't know what to do, but
Lye just looked at me and told me in her own
way that she would not let any harm come to
me or my girls. Then she made enough noise
to scare the burglars away, even after one of
them gave her a vicious kick as he fled.*

Lye's heroic actions have won her national recognition.
She was runner-up in the Heroic Hearing Dog of the
Year Awards in 2008, and she was chosen to appear in a
calendar being issued by a national dog magazine. Lye has

progressed from being a much-loved pet dog to being an invaluable lifeline.

Nicola summed it up: 'Lye is my constant and faithful companion, and a very special dog. She is my ears and she has given me back my confidence and courage.'

HEARING DOGS

In 1975, Agnes McGrath and the Minnesota Society for the Prevention of Cruelty to Animals developed a hearing dog programme which led to the establishment of the first institution training dogs for hearing-impaired people: International Hearing Dog, Inc. was founded in the UK in 1982, with the aim to 'offer greater independence, confidence and security to deaf people by providing dogs trained to alert them to chosen everyday sounds.'

Hearing assistance dogs go through three to 12 months' training before they are assigned to a hearing-impaired person. They can be of any breed, provided they pass an initial assessment, which checks whether they have the right temperament, are reactive to sounds and willing to work. If they fulfil these criteria, they receive obedience training and are taught how to act in various public scenarios, such as in a lift or on public transport and how to interact with different types of people.

After their 'social' training they move on to sound alerting. They are taught to give their handler a physical alert on hearing certain sounds, such as doorbells, smoke alarms, ringing telephones, sirens and a person calling the handler's name. They may also be trained to lead their handler away from a warning sound such as a fire alarm. The dogs are easily recognisable by their distinctive burgundy jackets, which helps to identify their handler's otherwise 'invisible' disability.

HAATCHI

A rescued three-legged dog helped a young disabled boy become more confident and overcome his fear of strangers...

It would be easy to imagine that a dog who had to have a hind leg and his tail amputated after being callously tied to a railway track would never trust anyone again. But Haatchi's story has a happy ending involving not only him but also a little boy with a rare genetic disorder.

The Anatolian shepherd dog was due to be put down after being found injured on the railway line, but instead was rescued by a charity and later rehomed by the Howkins family of Basingstoke, Hampshire, UK. Almost instantly, Will Howkins realized that there was a remarkable bond between his seven-year-old son Owen, who suffers from Schwartz-Jampel syndrome, and the three-legged dog.

'It seemed like there was a magical connection between the two of them where they knew something was different between each other – Owen didn't know what was wrong with Haatchi, and vice versa.'

Owen's condition means that his muscles are permanently tense, and as a result, he has to use a wheelchair. He said:

> *Haatchi has changed my life… I used to be scared of strangers, then Haatchi came along and now I'm not and that's how he changed my life. I didn't really meet many others with disabilities and felt like the odd one out, which made me really sad. But when I saw Haatchi and saw how strong he was, even though he only had three legs, I became stronger myself. I love him so much.*

Owen loves to tell their amazing story to passers-by while the two of them are out walking, bringing emotional tears to many an eye! Haatchi won the 2013 Crufts Friends for Life Award, based on a public vote, for his life-changing friendship with Owen.

BELLA AND FRODO

*Lizzie Owen, who suffered from Brittle Bone
Disease, felt that her two assistance dogs
had made her life worth living...*

Lizzie has a condition called Osteogenesis imperfecta, also
known as Brittle Bone Disease – with the result that she has
had about two hundred fractures and over 20 operations to
repair broken bones.

> *Due to my condition, I am rather short of
> stature, measuring just 3 feet 4 inches, and
> I am a wheelchair user. My father died in
> 1994, aged just 46, and since then, I've had
> spells of quite severe depression. I also get
> frustrated with my own health; I have one
> fracture after another, and can't make plans
> for the future. At times, I've wanted to end
> my life. However, simply by being there, my
> dogs have stopped me from doing anything
> drastic – I couldn't leave them behind!*

Lizzie would often fracture her ribs when she bent down to
pick things up and, after learning about the charity Dogs
for the Disabled, it occurred to her that having an assistance
dog to help out might save her from having so many painful
fractures. In the summer of 2000, Lizzie was partnered with
her first Dog for the Disabled. Bella was a lovely little golden
retriever with a gentle nature, and she and Lizzie achieved

some great things together: not only would Bella assist Lizzie in practical ways – picking things up and helping her to get dressed, for instance – she also provided a much-needed confidence boost for her, and in 2004, Lizzie graduated from the University of Leicester with a BSc in Physiology and Pharmacology.

'Without Bella, I don't think I would have been able to do it. When the coursework was piling up and I was ready to quit, Bella was there to give me a nudge in the right direction. Bella gave me confidence.'

Towards the end of her degree, Lizzie became quite depressed, concerned about what the future had in store for her – she was just about to leave education for the first time in 25 years. For a time, she and Bella worked at Leicestershire Centre for Integrated Living, a local disability organisation. However, due to an increased fracture rate, Lizzie had to resign from this job, and began to feel despondent again.

'I felt really down, but Bella was always there with her smiling face and wagging tail to pick me up again.'

In December 2007, when Bella was ten years old, she was diagnosed with inoperable cancer, and Lizzie had to have her faithful dog put to sleep. Lizzie hated having to make the decision to let her dog go, but poor Bella was in agony every minute of the day and, sadly, it was for the best.

> *She wasn't smiling, she wasn't wagging her tail, she was off her food – she was a very poorly little girl. I had Bella cremated, and her ashes are now buried in her favourite spot in Mum's garden. After Bella died, I wasn't sure if I could 'love' another dog again. If I couldn't love it, how could I*

work effectively with another Dog for the
Disabled? However, if I didn't have a dog,
what did I have?

Just before Christmas that year, Lizzie went to visit friends and family in Yorkshire, where she stayed with her stepfather's friend and his family. She spent most of her stay playing with their dog, Meg, and realised that she could love, live with and, most importantly, work with another dog.

In March 2008, Lizzie was partnered with her second Dog for the Disabled – Frodo, a two-year-old golden Labrador retriever.

'Frodo is a great young dog!' says Lizzie. 'His task work is superb! Not only does he pick things up for me and stop me from fracturing quite so many ribs, he also empties the washing machine, turns on lights, opens doors, picks up the post and helps me to undress. He's also a big comedian!'

When Lizzie fractured her right femur it wasn't healing, so she had to have surgery, which was not straightforward due to her poor bone quality. Unfortunately, it affected her mobility and Lizzie became quite depressed following the surgery. But Frodo had a gift for making her laugh by clowning around and prevented Lizzie's depression from deepening. On the days when she felt down and didn't want to get out of bed, he cheered her up with his antics.

Frodo also carried out the crucial role of enabling Lizzie to live independently in an adapted bungalow in Leicestershire. As well as his assistance dog duties, Frodo acted as a guard dog, and was always on hand in case Lizzie had a fall.

Frodo is such a laid-back dog and nothing
seems to faze him. I'm looking forward to

what the future has in store for Frodo and me – maybe we'll do our Masters, hopefully we'll return to work. I may even get Frodo a passport so that we can go over to France! What I do know is that we'll have lots of fun together! Without my dogs, I would have had many more rib fractures, I believe that I wouldn't have got my degree, and I probably wouldn't be alive today.

HANNAH

As a woman struggled to survive in a frightening world, tormented by her own demons, a young Staffie cross became her loyal companion, only leaving once there was a glimmer of light at the end of the dark tunnel...

Alice hoped her quest for a beagle was about to end the day she visited the Round Rock Humane Society animal shelter in Texas, USA. She'd had one when she was growing up, and always told herself that was the breed she'd have again, in memory of Sammie. But there was no beagle there. Instead, she fell instantly for a four-month-old Staffordshire bull terrier cross who didn't even have a name, but who looked deep into her eyes, and in that moment their future together was sealed. Alice named her Hannah, and she quickly became her soulmate.

Alice suffered from increasingly debilitating obsessive compulsive disorder (OCD), a neurological condition that made the world a scary place to be in and to try to cope with.

Although she didn't get Hannah as a therapy dog, the brindle Staffie cross seemed to understand from the very start that she would have a crucial role to play in her beloved human's life. The unconditional love, the unshakeable trust and loyalty, the rock-solid companionship – all this from Hannah helped Alice through the darkest, bleakest ten years of her life.

Halfway through this period, unable to afford the high cost of treatment for her condition in the USA, Alice returned to her home country of England. Hannah was able to join her three months later, once paperwork and the practicalities of transporting a dog across the Atlantic had been sorted out, and then had to put up with six months in quarantine, but she adored eventually being reunited with her much-loved human and luxuriating in the far more comfortable climate.

Over the next five years, Alice tried every treatment imaginable for OCD, none of which helped very much, but had undesirable side effects, including weight gain. Hannah remained by her side every step of the way, loving, gentle, undemanding and protective as Alice's quest to find a way through the OCD continued.

But one night in 2004, the Staffie cross, now ten, suddenly became very lethargic and collapsed. Alice rushed her to the vet, who found severe internal bleeding, probably due to an undiagnosed tumour on her spleen. Just as Alice and the vet were deciding whether to operate, Hannah passed away on the examination table.

Utterly bereft and devastated, Alice feared her world would fall apart without her soulmate companion by her side. But nine months later, a miracle happened. A new drug came on the market, rarely used to treat OCD, but it was prescribed for Alice in a last-ditch attempt to stave off brain surgery, such was the severity of her condition. Within days of taking the first tablet, the continuous-loop tape that seemed to be playing inside her head switched off, and she no longer felt compelled to keep checking everything obsessively. The excess weight fell off, and within four months she was applying for work again, having lived on benefits for six years. Within two years she was driving again.

Alice had her life back. But for the ten years she had so desperately needed a solid companion to guide her through the darkness, she had beside her the most faithful friend she would ever have in her life.

ROZ

Guide dog Roz was determined to carry out her duties for her owner, despite having been badly injured in a brutal attack...

The inspirational and moving story behind guide dog Roz, a Labrador–golden retriever cross, began when she was out guiding her blind owner Gary Wickett near his home in Great Barr, Birmingham, UK. As the pair made their way down a street in the area, three-year-old Roz was suddenly savaged by a large dog, in a sustained and horrific attack.

Gary, who was unable to prevent the attack or try to help Roz to defend herself from the much more aggressive dog, said: 'Being totally blind, I felt completely powerless and could do nothing more than to hold tightly on to Roz's lead.'

The owner of the attacking dog did not try to help or stop it from happening, and when the dog eventually finished its attack and was brought under control, the owner fled the scene without offering any assistance to Gary or Roz.

Despite suffering from horrendous injuries and bleeding heavily, Roz still managed to safely guide her owner Gary the half mile home so that he was able to call for help for her. She was lucky to be alive, and it was thought that she would have to retire due to physical injuries that included four severe bite wounds, 13 smaller wounds and a badly damaged tail, as well as the mental trauma she would have suffered in the incident.

However, after hours in surgery having her injuries tended to and following many weeks of rest and recuperation, Roz was back guiding Gary to his workplace in the busy centre of Birmingham. She was able to walk with confidence down the same road where the attack took place, loyally providing Gary with life-transforming independence and freedom.

Although a police investigation followed, the owner and dog involved in Roz's attack were not found.

Roz was crowned Overall Champion Guide Dog of the Year 2007 by the Guide Dogs for the Blind Association.

A HISTORY OF
LEADING THE BLIND

Dogs are thought to have been used to guide the blind since at least as far back as the mid-eighteenth century. During World War One, the first guide dog training schools were set up in Germany with the aim of helping returning soldiers who were blinded in combat to regain mobility. Britain's first guide dogs were German shepherds, and the first three trained were given to veterans blinded in World War One. In 1929, the first US guide dog school, The Seeing Eye, was founded in Morristown, New Jersey, and in 1934, the Guide Dogs for the Blind Association was set up in the UK, with the objective of providing 'guide dogs and other mobility services that increase the independence and dignity of blind and partially sighted people.'

Labradors, golden retrievers and German shepherds are the breeds most often used as guide dogs, and training starts when they are a year old. They learn the skills that are needed to keep a blind or partially sighted person safe in the outside world, such as walking in a straight line in the centre of the pavement unless there is an obstacle; not to turn corners unless told to do so; to stop at kerbs and wait for the command to cross the road, or to turn left or right; to judge height and width so that their owner does not bump their head or shoulder; how to deal with traffic. Their working life is around seven years, after which they retire, often staying on in the family's home as a much-loved pet.

CHAPTER 7

WHEN DISASTER STRIKES

If you live anywhere near a fault line, you'd be well advised to listen to what your dog is telling you, as dogs can sense an earthquake several crucial seconds before humans are able to notice that anything out of the ordinary is happening, giving them time to alert their owners so that they can get themselves and their loved ones to a safer space.

How they are able to do this is a mystery, but it may be that dogs can feel the P (primary) waves that are sent out by the shifting tectonic plates just before the S (seismic) waves occur that do the actual 'quaking'. Alternatively, there may be a chemical released just prior to the earthquake that dogs, with their highly sensitive noses, can detect. Or there may be an atmospheric shift that canines, more sensitive than humans, can sense.

It may be any or all of these things, or possibly something else entirely, but as this selection of stories shows, having your canine best friend by your side when disaster strikes could well be the thing that saves you!

DELTA

The deep devotion of many dogs towards their beloved humans is not a new thing. Stark and touching evidence dating back 2,000 years shows that a pet dog called Delta, doomed to perish along with her young owner in the volcanic eruption that destroyed the ancient Roman city of Pompeii, was brave and selfless to the very end...

The thick carpet of hot volcanic ash that rapidly entombed thousands of inhabitants of Pompeii in AD 79, along with many animals, encased their bodies in such a way that, in more recent years, it was found that startlingly lifelike casts could be made of the victims by pouring plaster into the holes left in the compacted ash by their long-decayed bodies. Among the curled-up victims discovered in this way was a young boy – and over him, the protective body of his faithful pet dog. An engraved metal disc also found in the hole showed that the dog was named Delta and the boy was called Severinus.

From the disc it is also known that Delta had saved her beloved young master's life not once, but three times before the eruption took both their lives. The first time, she saved him from drowning by pulling him out of the sea; next, she fought off four robbers who tried to steal from him; and then she saved him from an attack by a wolf near the city of Herculaneum.

When Pompeii was so rapidly covered by the hot ash erupting out of nearby Mount Vesuvius, no one had a chance to escape. But the hopelessness of the situation didn't stop Delta from doing her utmost to try to save Severinus a fourth time by lying on top of him and trying to shield him. Her devotion beyond death is preserved in the poignant plaster cast that has been made of the two bodies, joined together forever.

HERO

A German shepherd with wandering ways
gained a new name and a new owner through
saving the life of a complete stranger...

Shannon Lorio nearly lost her life after racing her car along a notoriously dangerous stretch of road in Georgia, USA and then crashing on a bend, following a row with her husband. She probably would have died, if a footloose German shepherd hadn't miraculously leapt to her rescue.

After the car tumbled backwards down an embankment, Shannon ended up sprawled on the boot, but too badly injured to make her way any further from the wreckage, which was so far from the road that it wouldn't be spotted by any passing motorists.

'I was bleeding from my face and my nose,' she said. 'All of a sudden, I felt a presence – a really huge presence. He [the German shepherd] was straddling me. I have watched too many horror movies about werewolves and vampires. I thought he was going to eat me.'

Instead, the dog seemed to instinctively know what to do, licking the semi-conscious woman's bloodied face clean and then dragging her 100 metres to the road, where he let her lever herself up with her arms around his strong neck in order to flag down the next car that came by.

After Shannon told the driver what had happened and asked him to phone her husband, she blacked out and only came round again in the hospital. She was told there that she had suffered an intracranial haemorrhage, which could have been fatal if she hadn't been able to get it treated in time.

An emotional Shannon said: 'This dog, he did everything. He's an amazing animal, he really is. I honestly believe, in my heart, that if he hadn't have… I probably wouldn't be here today. I really wouldn't. I think I honestly… I would have died. I really do.'

Because of his tendency to keep wandering off, following the accident the heroic dog's previous owners sadly signed him over to the local rescue centre, where he was aptly named Hero. But his story had a happy ending too, with at least 50 people offering to adopt him, including Heidy Drawdy, a search and rescue trainer who gave him a new home after seeing his potential to be a wilderness search and rescue dog – a job in which he would be likely to save many more lives in addition to Shannon's!

'He saved my life without any training,' said Shannon. 'And to think what he could do with the right amount of training, he could be saving many more lives. I told him, "You'll always be my hero."'

MAXX

A brave German shepherd risked his life to save two young children trapped inside a smoke-filled burning house...

When the Feaser family's house suddenly burst into flames one night following an explosion on the back porch, their loyal dog Maxx risked his life to save their two young children.

Neighbours saw the family's house in Longwood, Florida, USA go up in smoke late one evening in April 2016, and were horrified to realise that Margot and Brent Feaser and their 2- and 4-year-old children were all inside.

Although firefighters, together with help from the neighbours, managed to get both of the adults out, reaching the children was more difficult. Margot, herself an investigator with the Sheriff's Department in Seminole County desperately tried to re-enter the building to reach them, but was pulled back by the fire crew. It was then that Maxx, the family's German shepherd, sprang to the rescue.

By then the whole house was filled with smoke, making locating the children's bedrooms even more difficult. But Maxx fearlessly ran into the inferno and guided the firemen through the smoke to each of the children, suffering the effects of smoke inhalation as a result of his brave action.

The Feasers all suffered serious injuries from the fire and were taken to the local hospital, where they were stabilised. Maxx, the children's courageous saviour, was treated for the smoke inhalation by a vet and underwent minor surgery. A fund was set up to help cover the $75,000 bill for his treatment, that of the family, and other costs resulting from the fire. But without the pet dog's selfless determination to save his beloved young charges, the story could have had a much more tragic outcome.

FIREFIGHTING DOGS

In the USA, Dalmatians are traditionally known as firefighters' mascots – but it's a tradition that actually began in eighteenth-century England, and that originally had nothing to do with fire-fighting!

When it was realised that Dalmatians would run alongside and keep pace with horses, British aristocrats in the early 1700s started using them in pairs, one on either side of their coaches, as they would defend the horses from other dogs or anything that could frighten or attack them during the ride. Soon they became a status symbol – the more dogs you had running beside your carriage, the higher your social standing.

The use of Dalmatians in this way then carried over to the early horse-drawn fire wagons, with the dogs barking when a fire alarm sounded, and then running out of the firehouse to let passers-by know that the fire wagon was about to come out and that they needed to get out of the way.

Their presence at the scene of the fire served to calm down the horses that pulled the wagon, as horses are notoriously afraid of fire. In addition, the Dalmatians guarded the firefighters' belongings, ensuring that no one stole anything from the wagon while the crew were putting out the blaze.

When motorised vehicles came along, the use of Dalmatians by firemen didn't die out, although it altered somewhat. They became the fire crew's friendly companions, riding inside the fire engine instead of running alongside, and even catching and killing rats in the firehouses.

DORADO

To have been inside the World Trade Center on 11 September 2001 when the towers were hit by hijacked planes must have been a terrifying ordeal. For a blind man it must have been even more distressing. Luckily for Omar Eduardo Rivera, his faithful friend and guide dog Dorado was there to guide him out of danger...

Computer technician Omar was sitting at his desk with his guide dog, four-year-old Labrador Dorado, at his feet on the seventy-first floor of the north tower when the plane crashed into the building 25 floors above. As chaos ensued in the office, Omar could hear the sound of glass shattering around him and people screaming and fleeing. Smoke began to fill his lungs and the heat was quickly becoming unbearable.

Being unable to see, he knew that his chances of getting down the stairs past all the fallen obstacles and panicking people were pretty slim, and so he resigned himself to his fate. He let Dorado off his leash and ordered him to go, in the hope that at least the dog would make it out alive. At that moment Dorado was swept away by the crowds of pushing people, and Omar found himself alone.

But then, only a few minutes later, Omar felt a familiar nudging against his knee. His faithful guide had returned.

Dorado guided his master to the stairwell, where a co-worker recognised Omar. With his co-worker on his right and Dorado on his left, Omar was safely guided down 70 flights of stairs and out into the street. Because of the sheer volume of people on the stairs, it took them nearly an hour to get out, with Dorado nudging Omar reassuringly every step of the way.

It was only moments after they made it out onto the street that the tower collapsed. 'I owe my life to Dorado,' Omar later said, 'my companion and best friend.'

ROSELLE

Michael Hingson is another blind person who was in the World Trade Center when the terrorist attacks happened...

A golden Labrador and guide dog called Roselle led Michael Hingson down 78 floors and out of the World Trade Center after the planes hit. But her work didn't end there – she still had to get Michael safely home. When they were about two blocks away from the building, the first tower began to collapse. Amongst all the chaos Roselle remained calm as they ran for the shelter of the subway. When they re-emerged, the second tower collapsed, covering them with ash. But Roselle still remained calm, and guided Michael to the home of one of his friends, where he was able to wait in safety until the trains were back in action, then travel home to his worried wife. Since then Michael has become a motivational speaker, drawing on his experience with Roselle that day when he speaks to audiences about trust and teamwork.

BRETAGNE

The last surviving dog to be involved in the traumatic 9/11 search and rescue effort finally succumbed to kidney failure at the ripe old age of 16, after a lifetime of brave service...

Bretagne, a golden retriever, was just two when the aircraft crashed into the twin towers of the World Trade Center. But her owner Denise Corliss, who accompanied her to the site of the disaster for her first ever search and rescue mission, said that although at first she herself felt overwhelmed by its scale, Bretagne just looked eager to work, despite the gruelling 12-hour shifts.

As well as using their noses to detect people who were still alive but trapped underneath the rubble, the 300 first responder dogs spurred the human workers on by their very presence, according to Cindy Otto, a vet who looked after 100 of the dogs involved in the 9/11 search and rescue mission.

'You'd see firefighters sitting there, unanimated, stone-faced, no emotion, and then they'd see a dog and break out into a smile. Those dogs brought the power of hope. They removed the gloom for just an instant,' she said, adding, 'Bretagne's partnership with Denise Corliss was magical.'

In subsequent years, Bretagne assisted in the rescue efforts following Hurricane Katrina, Hurricane Ivan and Hurricane Rita, and she was also a therapy dog, regularly visiting a local elementary school and working with autistic children.

On Bretagne's sixteenth birthday, she and Denise visited Ground Zero, the site of the destroyed buildings where they had assisted in the rescue effort so many years previously.

In June 2016, touchingly, a row of firefighters saluted the elderly heroine, who had received many honours throughout her life in recognition of her bravery, as she made her final journey to the Fairfield Animal Hospital in Cypress, Texas.

Though Bretagne passed away, her incredible legacy lives on – not least in the diabetes assistance dog who was named after her: Bretagne 2.

DID YOU KNOW?
FACTS ABOUT THE 9/11 RESCUE DOGS

During the chaos of the 9/11 attacks in 2001, in which nearly 3,000 people died, between 300 and 900 brave search and rescue dogs and their equally courageous handlers scoured the rubble of Ground Zero for survivors. Most of those heroic dogs were Labradors or golden retrievers.

Following the tragedy, a study was conducted on the lives of the rescue dogs. Most of them were quite long-lived – on average they lived to be 12, and the last one, Bretagne, a golden retriever, died in 2016 at the age of 16. Although many of the dogs suffered from cancer towards the end of their lives, it was not thought to have been related to their participation in the

9/11 recovery mission; generally the cancer was consistent with the type of disease elderly dogs typically encounter.

The dogs were also found to have helped prevent Post-Traumatic Stress Disorder in their handlers.

EVE

Eve was a loyal pet Rottweiler who pulled her grateful owner Kathie to safety after a terrible accident...

Kathie Vaughn had just bought a used truck and was driving back to her home in Indiana, USA that morning when it started to weave erratically across the road. *So much for the great deal on the truck*, she thought, as she managed to get the steering back on course, but then as she braked, there was a loud screech and the interior quickly began to fill with toxic fumes.

The fact that she was paralysed from the waist down meant that she was trapped in a vehicle that was at risk of blowing up, with no way of getting out quickly. The smoke and fumes were getting thicker, preventing her from finding her wheelchair and assembling it.

Eve, her Rottweiler, was still sitting in the passenger seat. She managed to reach over and open the door to let the dog out to safety while she continued to fumble around in the heavy smoke. But Eve didn't go anywhere. Somehow, she knew what to do. The Rottweiler jumped back into the fume-filled truck, gripped Kathie's paralysed leg in her teeth, and dragged her out of the vehicle. The dog had pulled her three metres away from the truck when it exploded into flames. She continued to drag Kathie to a ditch to protect her from the terrifying blaze.

A policeman arrived soon after and, seeing the vehicle on fire, yelled at the woman to get further away. Kathie knew she had to drag herself away from danger, but didn't have the strength. Eve seemed to have used all her strength too, and lay still. But suddenly the exhausted dog got up determinedly, and let her owner hold tight on her collar while she dragged her another 12 metres away, where Kathie was safe and the policeman would be able to take over in her rescue.

But he couldn't, as Eve continued trying to protect her owner – this time from the policeman!

'Eve had to help me get to the police car,' explained Kathie, 'because she wouldn't let the policeman get to me. That's the true nature of the Rottweiler – they're very loyal and loving and will take care of their owners at all cost. She just loves me.'

HERO

Hero, a four-year-old golden retriever, lived up to his name when his owner found himself in a dangerous predicament in 2002...

Gareth Jones, of Caldicot in Monmouthshire, Wales, was involved in a car accident in 1995 and has been paralysed ever since. He uses a wheelchair to get out and about, and his assistance dog, Hero, was specially trained to help him in over 100 different tasks.

Gareth had taken Hero out for his daily exercise and some fresh air in the fields not far from their house one day when his wheelchair lost its grip in the muddy field and slipped, becoming stuck. No matter what Gareth did, he couldn't free the wheels and he began to wonder whether he would be able to get home – there was no one around to call for help and he felt very isolated and alone.

But luckily Hero was there and seemed to know exactly what to do. 'When I got stuck in the mud he realised I was in trouble, and started pulling on the rope I threw to him,' said Gareth. As Hero grasped the rope between his teeth and pulled with all his might, the wheels slowly began to grip again and the wheelchair started to move out of the mud. 'He didn't let go until I was clear – he knew exactly what he was doing.'

Hero was later presented with an outstanding achievement award for his actions at the All-Star Animal Awards in London by Ann Widdecombe, at that time an MP. The plucky pooch is said to have solemnly offered the MP a paw to shake!

CHAPTER 8

DOGS OF WAR

Specially trained dogs have been used in military combat since Roman times, and the Romans are said to have had attack formations made up solely of dogs. In World War One, European armies used ambulance dogs to help locate wounded soldiers on the battlefield and the British Army also trained up special messenger, sentry and guard dogs.

The first ever 'disaster' rescue dogs were employed in London during the air raids of World War Two and the Americans also started an official war dog programme in 1944, with more than 10,000 dogs (known as the K-9 Corps) enlisted for training over the course of the war.

In the late twentieth and early twenty-first centuries, dogs have been used for a variety of purposes by military staff in Bosnia, Iraq and Afghanistan among other hotspots, where they have been used for sniffing out bombs and mines, detecting illegal weapons at border crossings, tracking suspected insurgents and subduing detainees.

A number of special awards have been created to honour the important role played by these courageous dogs and other animals in war zones around the world, some of whose stories are told in this chapter.

VALDO

A courageous naval working dog retired after
taking the brunt of an exploding rocket propelled
grenade and saving four lives in the process...

When Valdo the German shepherd went with his handler, Navy Petty Officer 2nd Class Ryan Lee, to sniff out roadside bombs in Afghanistan, life was never going to be easy.

The pair took part in Operation Red Sand, attached to 7th Squadron, 10th Cavalry Regiment, and on 4 April 2011 their patrol came under heavy enemy fire in a field in the Bala Murghab district of Badghis province. When one of the many rocket propelled grenades (RPGs) being targeted at them exploded in the middle of Valdo's group, Valdo used his large German shepherd frame to shield the soldiers and take the brunt of the explosion. He was seriously injured, but his tough canine skin and thick fur saved his life, and as a result of his brave action, the four soldiers around him only sustained minor injuries from the shrapnel.

'If Valdo wasn't here, I'm pretty sure I'd be dead right now,' said Private Ben Bradley, one of the soldiers who had been just feet from Valdo and who was fortunate only to sustain minor injuries during the attack that nearly cost Valdo his life.

Lee said:

> *That was a handler's worst nightmare. When*
> *that RPG came in and exploded next to us,*
> *all I could think about was how to get Valdo*
> *off that field. His screams were jolting and*

*I knew I had to get him to safety, and felt
helpless because there was nothing I could
do with the amount of incoming fire.*

Lee carried Valdo nearly a mile and a half to a military
outpost, where he was treated by an army medic before
being evacuated from the battle area and sent to a camp in
Herat for further treatment.

Valdo underwent five operations and eventually recovered
from his serious injuries, but his military career was at an end.
The brave dog was awarded a Purple Heart for his courageous
work in one of the world's most dangerous hotspots.

ROCKET

*A brave military service dog risked his life
in a dangerous burning building…*

Rocket was a courageous member of the K-9 assault dogs
unit of the Indian National Security Guard (NSG) who
specialised in detecting the presence of humans, explosives
and improvised explosive devices (IEDs). He played a life-
saving role during counter-terrorist operations at Pathankot
Air Force Station, part of the Western Air Command of the
Indian Air Force, in January 2016.

After a group of Jaish-e-Mohammad militants set fire to the
base, causing 53 explosions in structures where ammunition
and inflammable material had been stored, Rocket, a Belgian
Malinois specially bred by the NSG, was sent into an airmen's

billet to determine whether terrorists were still alive inside. The building was burning so fiercely that it was decided that the Black Cat commandos could not enter after seven soldiers lost their lives in the blaze.

Rocket came out with a burnt pouch in his mouth. It had belonged to one of the Fedayeen guerrillas, and security personnel then entered the building, in which they found the dead terrorist's burned body.

Rocket suffered severe burns to his paws and head, but after lengthy treatment made a full recovery and returned to action. He received a Gallantry Award for his bravery.

JET

Over 100 people owed their lives to the nose of one brave dog who worked tirelessly throughout the London Blitz during World War Two...

A fearless dog's life-saving exploits during World War Two were so incredible that they were featured in a 2015 exhibition commemorating the London Blitz.

Jet, who was born in Liverpool, UK in 1942 and was highly trained in anti-sabotage work as well as search and rescue duties at the War Dogs School in Gloucester, worked in London with his handler, Corporal Wardle, during the most intense period of bombing in 1944.

It was the black German shepherd's finely tuned sense of smell, as well as his lack of fear, that enabled him to detect survivors even in smoke-filled buildings. Where many dogs are afraid of fire, Jet was so keen to enter burning buildings that he often had to be held back, and through his bravery he saved over 100 people from bombed buildings during the Blitz.

Among those he rescued was an elderly lady trapped on a ledge in the ruins of a Chelsea hotel that had been thoroughly searched already. The rescue crew assumed there were no more survivors in the buildings, but Jet kept going back to a particular section of a wall that was on the point of falling over. It was his insistence that led one of the rescuers to climb it very carefully and find the old lady on the ledge.

Jet received the Dickin Medal (the animal equivalent of the Victoria Cross) on 12 January 1945 for his actions, with the inscription on the award reading: 'For being responsible for the rescue of persons trapped under blitzed buildings while serving with the Civil Defence Services of London.'

But the end of the war didn't spell the end of Jet's exploits or honours. After he returned to his owner in Liverpool, he was involved in the rescue of several miners in 1947 following a pit explosion in Cumbria, for which he received the RSPCA's Medallion of Valour.

After the heroic dog died in 1949, a memorial was built close to where he was buried at Calderstones Park in Liverpool.

THE DICKIN MEDAL

The Dickin Medal for animals showing gallantry or devotion to duty was first awarded during and just after World War Two. Regarded globally as the animal equivalent of the Victoria Cross, the highest military honour, it was established in the UK by Maria Dickin, the founder of the PDSA, and between 1943 and 1949 it was awarded 54 times – to 32 pigeons, 18 dogs, three horses and one cat.

In 2000 it was revived in order to honour Gander, a Newfoundland dog who died in the act of saving the lives of several Canadian infantrymen during the Battle of Lye Mun on Hong Kong Island in December 1941. Since then, it has been awarded to a number of dogs, some of whom responded to the 9/11 attacks or served in Bosnia-Herzegovina or Iraq.

More recently, it was awarded posthumously to Diesel, a seven-year-old Belgian shepherd police dog who died on 18 November 2015 in a shoot-out five days after the Paris terrorist attacks which killed 130 people.

GABE

A former rescue dog went on to have a glittering military career and in his retirement raised funds for his active canine comrades...

Embarking on his courageous army career after being rescued from a Texas animal shelter, a military dog continued his noble work even after he had retired from active duty.

Gabe, who spent several years as a sniffer dog in Iraq, raised thousands of dollars for his comrades by winning a national Hero Dog title, the prize money from which was donated to the United States War Dogs Association, which sends out care packages to US military working dogs and their handlers. These packages include ear muffs and dog booties for the paws of the military dogs.

Gabe was paired with his handler, Sergeant Charles 'Chuck' Shuck, in 2006, and went on more than 200 dangerous combat missions in Iraq, sniffing out insurgent bombs, guns and ammunition. The largest of his 26 'finds' during the combat patrols he was involved in was a huge cache of rounds on the banks of the Tigris River.

Gabe retired in 2009 at the rank of Sergeant First Class, when he was adopted by Shuck, having been honoured for his service with three Army Commendation Medals, an Army Achievement Medal from each of the different units, and dozens of coins of excellence. In 2008, he also received the Heroic Military Working Dog Award Medal from the American Kennel Club.

Gabe went on to become the American Humane Association's 2012 Hero Dog, competing with 358 other dogs, including therapy dogs, law enforcement dogs, emerging hero dogs, service dogs, guide dogs, hearing dogs, military dogs and search and rescue dogs.

Although Gabe sadly passed away from liver cancer less than a year later, the title had made him a celebrity and raised the profile of the work carried out by courageous military dogs in war-torn parts of the world.

SERGEANT BODO

*Joaquin Mello was on assignment in Iraq with K-9
Sergeant Bodo when an unsettling incident made
the reality of war really hit home for him...*

US K-9 Handler Specialist Joaquin Mello from Santa Cruz
in California was in Iraq in 2009 with the 98th Military
Police Company. He and a dog handler from the Air Force
were completing a route-clearing mission near the town of
Najaf ahead of a convoy and were required to clear some
suspicious rubble, which meant leaving the protection of the
Mine Resistant Ambush Protected (MRAP) vehicle.

The pair divided up the task so that Mello would clear
ahead of the convoy and the airman behind it. Mello and his
dog, Sgt. Bodo, a six-year-old German shepherd trained in
explosives detection, set to work together. Mello noticed that
Bodo was behaving oddly.

'I had Bodo on the retractable leash and while we were
searching he started to get a little bit behind me so I tried
to coach him ahead of me but he wouldn't go and I ended
up getting in front of him,' said Mello, who knew by this
unusual behaviour that something was bothering the dog.
He leaned down to put his head close to ground level to
listen, then gave the dog the order to seek. Strangely, Bodo
didn't immediately comply.

'All of a sudden he jerked sharply behind me and him
jerking the leash jerked my head up,' said Mello. 'I heard a
whiz and a loud ping like metal hitting rock. Sand started
kicking up in my face and I'm waving my hands because I

can't see because I have dust in my eyes. Then it hit me like a ton of bricks – someone just shot at me.'

Mello had been completely unaware of the enemy close by and had no idea where the bullet had come from. The gunners realised what had happened and shouted to Mello to get back into the MRAP vehicle but he was momentarily blinded by the sand, so a soldier helped him to safety.

The bullet had landed only a foot in front of where he had been listening with his head to the ground. 'That was a scary day for me... If Bodo hadn't pulled me back it would have hit me right in the head.'

The likeliest explanation, according to Mello, for the dog's swift action was his powerful sense of hearing.

'He can hear things we can't. He will hear things before I hear them too, he lifts his head up, his ears perk up,' said Mello. 'It's possible he did hear the round and thought "Dad's in trouble" and pulled me back... All I know is Bodo, without a doubt, saved my life that day.'

Mello was badly shaken by the experience, acknowledging that it was the first moment when the true reality of war actually hit him. Back in his unit, leadership asked him if he wanted to be nominated for a Combat Action Badge after his close brush with fatal gunfire, but he declined.

'I just did my job. Bodo is the one who did something amazing.' Joaquin Mello will never forget the day his working dog Bodo saved his life.

CHIPS

*Probably the most famous and certainly the most
decorated military dog was Chips, one of the first
dogs in the K-9 Corps to be shipped overseas
by the US Army during World War Two...*

Dogs for Defense (DFD) was set up in the USA after the attack on Pearl Harbor during World War Two. The Armed Forces needed dogs, and thousands of patriotic pet owners across America responded by donating their dogs for enlistment into the K-9 Corps.

Chips was a German shepherd–collie–husky mix, and was donated by Edward J. Wren of Pleasantville, New York, to the K-9 Corps. Quick to learn, he was trained to be a sentry dog at the War Dog Training Center at Front Royal, Virginia, in 1942. Assigned to the 3rd Infantry Division, he would travel with that unit in North Africa, Italy, France and Germany with handler Private John P. Rowell.

One of Chips' first and most prestigious duties was to serve as a sentry dog for the Roosevelt–Churchill conference in January 1943. He was also credited as having been directly responsible for the capture of numerous enemy soldiers by alerting troops to their presence. On one occasion, Chips alerted his unit to an impending ambush then ran back to base with a phone cable attached to his collar, dodging enemy gunfire, so that the endangered platoon could set up a communications line to ask for the backup they so desperately needed.

During the 1943 invasion of Sicily, Chips and his handler were pinned down one morning on the beach by an enemy machine-gun team in a disguised pillbox. Chips broke free from his handler and lunged into the pillbox, attacking the gunners. He seized one man and all four Italian crewmen were forced to leave the pillbox and surrender to US troops. In the fight he sustained a scalp wound and powder burns, but later that night he returned to duty and helped take ten more Italians prisoner by alerting troops to their approach, giving enough advance warning for the squad to capture all of them.

For his actions during the war, he was awarded the Silver Star for Valor and a Purple Heart for his wounds, and was much lauded in the press; however, ironically it was the press attention that caused these awards to be revoked. The Commander of the Military Order of the Purple Heart complained to both President Roosevelt and the War Department that by so honouring Chips, they were demeaning all the men who had been awarded a Purple Heart. The dog lost his medals, but the unit unofficially awarded him a theatre ribbon with an arrowhead, signifying that he had taken part in an assault landing, and battle stars for each of his eight campaigns.

He was given an honourable discharge in December 1945 and returned to the Wren family in Pleasantville. In 1990, Disney made a TV movie based on his life entitled *Chips, the War Dog*.

JUDY

*British Royal Navy dog Judy was credited with
saving the lives of countless sailors during World
War Two, and became the only animal ever to
have been registered as a prisoner of war...*

Judy, an English pointer, was a ship's dog on a Royal Navy
vessel before and during World War Two, and gained a
reputation for her skills in warning troops of the approach of
hostile Japanese aircraft long before any of the human crew
could hear them. Pointers were bred as gun dogs and are
known for their alertness, and Judy saved the lives of sailors
on many occasions in this way.

When the vessel to which Judy was assigned sank during
a battle, its crew became prisoners of war. Judy somehow
managed to get into the camp, where the conditions were
terrible and the POWs had to work all day building a railway
with very little to eat. The dog found scraps of food, which
she would bring to the men, aiding their survival. The
Japanese prison guards tried to shoot her, but one of the men
came to her rescue, a Royal Air Force serviceman named
Frank Williams. He convinced the camp commandant to
register her as an official prisoner of war, with the number
'81A Gloergoer, Medan', and she was the only animal to be
registered in this way.

After the war, Judy's life was in danger once again when
she was about to be put to death by the Japanese guards
following a lice outbreak amongst the prisoners. Williams
hid her until the Allied forces arrived, and he and some others

smuggled her back to the UK aboard a troopship. She spent the next six months in quarantine, but was then adopted by Frank and awarded what was dubbed by the press as the Victoria Cross for animals, the Dickin Medal, introduced to honour animals that had made an outstanding contribution during the war.

The following citation received along with her medal stands in tribute to her achievements:

'For magnificent courage and endurance in Japanese prison camps, which helped to maintain morale among her fellow prisoners and also for saving many lives through her intelligence and watchfulness.'

Judy remained with Frank and died on 17 February 1960 in Tanzania, where Frank was working at the time. He buried her there, building a monument at her grave and attaching a large metal plaque recording Judy's life and all her courageous feats. Her collar and medal were displayed in the Imperial War Museum, London, in 2006 as part of the 'Animals' War' exhibition, and in the seventies a book was published by Edwin Varley and Wendy James entitled *The Judy Story: The Dog with Six Lives*.

BUSTER

*A brave springer spaniel saved countless
lives all over the world, making friends with
the local children at the same time...*

A valiant British military dog saved more than 1,000 lives by sniffing out lethal improvised explosive devises (IEDs), weapons and other ammunition in dangerous hotspots all over the world. Buster, a springer spaniel who completed five tours of duty in Bosnia, Iraq and Afghanistan, began working with Flight Sergeant Will Barrow in 2007, when the pair were deployed to Afghanistan's deadly Helmand province. Buster also patrolled British military bases in those war-torn countries and searched vehicles at checkpoints. Even in the face of enemy attacks, he remained unflappable.

'Each time [we were attacked], Buster waited calmly for the action to cease, then carried on his search for improvised explosive devices, and keeping patrols safe,' said Will Barrow. 'He saved my life every day we were together. I owe him so much.'

Buster used his highly sensitive nose to sniff out explosive vests, leading to the arrest of two suicide bombers, as well as being useful on the diplomatic front owing to his friendly disposition towards the local children.

When he retired he became the official RAF Police mascot and also continued his diplomatic mission, making appearances in schools in his local area of Lincolnshire, UK. Flt Sgt Barrow wrote a bestselling book – *Buster: The Military Dog Who Saved a Thousand Lives* – but sadly Buster passed away in July 2015 at the age of 13.

CHAPTER 9

SOUNDING THE ALARM

While she remains perhaps the most famous fictional dog hero character of all time, Lassie isn't the only dog with the ability to somehow sense danger and warn her human companions in time to save the day. This chapter features many real-life dog heroes who have raised the alarm when their owners were in trouble, or who have led would-be rescuers to someone who was in danger and needed help.

Whether these dogs are alerting their owners to the presence of intruders or to the fact that the house is burning down, or desperately barking in an effort to muster help for someone in need – their loved one or even a complete stranger – there's nothing fictitious about these incredible and selfless acts of canine heroism!

JADE

An abandoned newborn baby was saved by a German shepherd who heard her tiny cries from a carrier bag in the middle of a clump of bushes...

While out walking in the local park with her owner late in October 2013, nine-year-old German shepherd Jade ran over to what looked like a discarded carrier bag in a clump of bushes and lay down beside it, refusing to leave it until her owner, 68-year-old Roger Wilday, came over to investigate.

Mr Wilday, from Birmingham, UK, said: 'I walked over and saw a carrier bag – then I saw it move. I thought it was a bag of kittens, but then I saw her little arms and a head, and the baby started to cry.'

He immediately called the police and the baby, thought to be no more than 24 hours old and to have been there for around 30 minutes, was whisked off to hospital, where she made a full recovery within a few days.

But the story could have been so different had not Jade – who had never found anything significant before – made the discovery that day in the park.

Police Inspector Ian Green said: 'Paediatricians have confirmed the baby was lucky to be found when she was, as even just a few more hours exposed to the elements could have had fatal consequences.'

The Wildays put Jade's remarkable find down to her acute sense of hearing and her love of children.

Catherine Wilday, Roger's wife, said: 'She's very keen on our [five] grandchildren. Whenever she hears their names she whimpers. She just loves kids.'

Police continued to search for the mother of the baby, who was named Jade after her sharp-eared canine saviour.

DOUGIE

A Staffie suffering from canine epilepsy didn't let his own night-time demons prevent him from seeing off an early-morning intruder and alerting his family to the attempted break-in...

Dougie the Staffordshire bull terrier was just two years old when he started barking frantically in the early hours one morning in the summer of 2010. He was alerting his sleeping family – a mother and son – to the fact that a burglar had just climbed in through a ground-floor window at their home in Oxford, England. On hearing the savage barking, the burglar turned and fled.

Dougie's seemingly fearless behaviour that night belied the fact that nights were the most frightening time for him: a year before, he had suffered his first epileptic fit – in the middle of the night.

'I heard a bang and found him frothing under the coffee table,' said his owner, Jane.

When he came round from it, he was temporarily blind, as well as scared and incontinent. By the morning, he had bounced back to his normal self, but after that incident, night time was always the most difficult time for him.

For the rest of Dougie's tragically short life, the seizures struck on virtually a monthly basis, racking up £200 every month in medical bills and robbing the brave bull terrier of his sight and his dignity. To protect him from further harm that could have resulted from the violent fits, Jane even ended up letting him sleep on her bed while she slept on the floor!

When he was five, Dougie had a final massive fit that was too severe for him to recover from. But his seizure-ridden life never changed his gentle nature.

'Not once did he turn nasty or not enjoy life. He was a star!' said Jane proudly.

Dougie's kennel name was Biondi the Dark Knight, and on the night he saved his loved ones from the break-in, the dog who, during his short life, was beset by illness and fear, truly lived up to his chivalrous name!

DID YOU KNOW?
THERE ARE MANY OTHER REASONS BESIDES RAISING THE ALARM THAT DOGS BARK.

🐾 It can be rewarding – dogs can find it fun to bark, and if the postman leaves when they bark, or if you give them a treat or throw the ball when they bark, it simply encourages them to keep doing it because they know they'll get a reward for doing so!

🐾 Some breeds bark more than others – especially herding breeds that use it as an effective tool for their job.

🐾 They might be barking to protect their territory.

🐾 They might bark because they're happy to see people.

🐾 They might bark out of boredom.

🐾 They might bark to join in with other dogs barking.

🐾 They might bark out of frustration – if, for instance, their ball rolls under the couch out of reach.

🐾 It might be compulsive barking – this type of barking may be accompanied by running back and forth or spinning in circles, and is often linked to stress and anxiety.

🐾 The barking might be due to separation anxiety if the dog is left alone.

🐾 Behavioural techniques, altering the dog's surroundings, and giving the dog plenty of exercise and stimulation are methods that are often successfully used to stop undesirable barking.

🐾 The basenji, or African wolf dog, is the only dog in the world that is unable to bark.

HONEY

An abandoned cocker spaniel saved her new owner's life within days of being adopted by him...

Honey had taken a shine to Michael Bosch the moment he picked her up and cuddled her at the local animal rescue centre, and by day two of their life together at his home outside San Rafael, California, USA the five-month-old cocker spaniel was firmly bonded to him. By day three, she'd saved his life.

Michael's home was in a remote setting close to a steep ravine, which it took skill to avoid plunging down every time he reversed his car out of the driveway. On the second day after he'd adopted Honey, he decided to go for a drive into town, making sure he had his tablets for his heart condition with him. He decided to also take Honey along with him for the ride as his wife was away for a few days and he didn't want to leave her on her own so soon. Placing her in the passenger seat of his Toyota 4Runner, he reversed down the drive, but was suddenly blinded by the dazzling sun – and before he knew it, the worst had happened and the vehicle was tumbling down the slope, somersaulting over and over until it hit a tree and came to a halt.

Pinned down by a heavy branch that had come through the window, and feeling severe chest pains, he glanced over to the passenger seat and was relieved to see Honey still sitting there uninjured, though scared. He soon realised that he was in the most nightmarish position he could be in – his phone had no signal at the bottom of the cliff, the vehicle was too far down for anyone to spot the wreckage, and his neighbour Robin rarely came round to visit, and even if she did, she'd just assume he'd gone out somewhere.

All he was able to do was open his window a crack and squeeze Honey out – at least she could run to safety, even if he was doomed. Honey immediately scampered up the slope and was soon out of sight.

Hours went by and Michael had resigned himself to his fate – when suddenly he heard a car pull into the drive above. The horn wasn't working, so, summoning all his failing strength, he cried out, 'Help!'

The answer came back, 'Who needs help?' The voice belonged to Robin!

'It's me, Michael, I'm at the bottom of the ravine!'

Soon he was being airlifted to hospital, where he was found to have numerous broken ribs and internal bleeding, as well as an injured leg that would take a while to heal. But he was safe – and it was Honey who'd saved him!

Robin told him of how the little dog had come racing up her drive and run around in frantic circles, obviously highly agitated. She'd just assumed the newly adopted dog had got lost and had driven her home – at which point she'd heard his cry for help.

It hadn't taken the young cocker spaniel long to find a way to repay Michael for his kindness in giving her a loving new home – by saving his life!

LEALA

A vigilant Staffie saved her young owner's life and, in doing so, gained the lifelong admiration and respect of his relieved parents...

Alexander Kenney is only alive today because of the quick thinking of his ever-loyal companion, Staffordshire bull terrier Leala.

When nine-year-old Leala found her young owner floating unconscious in a fast-flowing dammed river in September 2015, the dog, who had an aversion to cold water, bravely leapt in to try to drag him to safety. But she found that she couldn't pull him out, so the gutsy little dog ran home for help, soaking wet, to alert the toddler's father by barking frantically at him when she got there.

David Kenney, who had taken his young son to visit friends who lived on the coast of New South Wales, Australia, when the accident happened, immediately realised that something was amiss and rushed with his friends to the dam, where he managed to get his son out of the water and perform resuscitation on him for 27 minutes before the paramedics arrived and airlifted the youngster to a hospital in Brisbane. Doctors there put him in an induced coma for 36 hours, but were convinced that Alexander, whose chances of surviving at all were slim to say the least, would be brain damaged if he did pull through, as his brain had been starved of oxygen for so long.

What actually happened was as incredible as Leala's life-saving feat had been. Within 48 hours, the little boy was making an amazing recovery, and he was able to breathe on his own after he was brought out of the induced coma. Remarkably, it wasn't long before he was able to go home, where he soon bounced back from his ordeal.

The doctors put this down to his father's prompt action once he arrived at the scene of the accident, and to Leala's amazing instinctive behaviour that had guided him there in the first place.

Lisa Brockbank, Alexander's grateful mother, said: 'Without [Leala] we wouldn't have our little boy with us today, Scotch fillets forever sweetheart!'

TRUE

A disabled dachshund repaid a young single mother for her kindness in giving him a loving home by saving her life and that of her baby...

When Katie Crosley adopted a dog from the local animal rescue centre that no one else had wanted – not only was he deaf and blind, he only had three legs – little did she know that the grateful dachshund would one day return the favour by saving her life and that of her baby boy. Her son, Jace, had been born with a heart defect and required a lot of medical attention, so her new pet dog, True, was in knowledgeable and caring hands.

Early one Sunday morning in November 2012, Katie and Jace were woken by the sound of True wailing loudly – a miracle in itself, considering his sensory disabilities. Katie thought he merely wanted to go outside, but when she opened the door to let him out, she realised that their cabin in Grady County, Oklahoma, USA was burning down around them.

The electrical fire had spread to the front porch by then, barricading the three of them inside. Although Katie managed to escape with Jace and True through the back of the cabin, all their belongings – including all of the baby supplies and all of Jace's medical records – were lost in the fire. However, they still had their lives – thanks to a severely disabled dog who had been rejected by everyone else.

DEXTER

*A Patterdale terrier found a memorable way
to thank his new owner for adopting him
from a rescue centre – by saving his life!*

Four months after being rescued from the Battersea Dogs Home at Brands Hatch in Kent, UK a small but lively black dog more than repaid his new owners for the favour – in a truly life-saving way!

While Iain was out walking his new rescue dog Dexter at the local park early in 2016, he was bitten by an insect and immediately collapsed with anaphylactic shock. With no one around to help, the outcome could easily have been tragic. But although Iain was unconscious and unaware of it at the time, his faithful new Patterdale terrier was doing all he could to revive him as well as to raise the alarm and get help for the stricken man.

The muddy paw prints all over Iain's shirt that were discovered later were a sure sign that the anxious dog had been frantically jumping up and down on his chest and licking his face in an effort to revive him, as well as barking until someone heard and came to their rescue.

Dexter's dogged persistence paid off, as someone eventually heard him and came to investigate. Soon an emergency crew and Iain's wife Jane were by Iain's side – to the relief of Dexter, who leapt into Jane's arms as soon as he saw her.

Iain made a full recovery – and as for his best pal and saviour Dexter, well, thanks to his heroic action that day at the park, he can't put a paw wrong these days!

BORIS

Many of the dogs in this book have received rewards for their acts of heroism, but Boris received something more unusual in recognition of his achievements – a rather special invitation...

John Richards was out for an evening walk his boxer dog, Boris, in the fields near their home in Ottery St Mary, Devon, UK in November 2004 when the dog suddenly ran off the path and stood by something he had discovered on the ground. John called him to heel but Boris refused. John continued to call him back, but Boris remained stubborn and it eventually began to dawn on John that the boxer was trying to convince him to look at what he had found, so, in the winter darkness, he went back to where his dog was standing to investigate. What he saw filled him with horror.

A young woman, blue with cold, lay in the field; she was lifeless and still, and John thought she must have been dead. He called for an ambulance and a police officer arrived on the scene as well. Following procedure, the officer checked to see whether the girl had a pulse while John looked on and to their astonishment she did, although it was incredibly weak. An air ambulance arrived to take her to hospital, during which time her heart stopped and she had to be resuscitated.

Eventually, after weeks in intensive care, 21-year-old Zoe Christie from Newton Poppleford, Devon made a full recovery from a severe case of hypothermia and was able to return to work as a care assistant. She was so grateful to Boris for saving her life that she invited him to her wedding as the guest of honour, where he received the applause and adulation of all the guests.

Zoe's dad Trevor said, 'She owes her life to that dog and his persistence.'

DOR

Koichi Wada's dog Dor seemed to have an uncanny
ability to sense when strangers were in danger...

Koichi Wada and his three-year-old black Labrador retriever Dor were out for a walk in Iwade, Japan, one day, when the dog started barking frantically at a parked car that was partly hidden under a bridge, prompting Wada to investigate – and then call the police, so worried had he become at what he had seen. Inside the car, the police found a middle-aged man who was getting ready to commit suicide by jumping off the bridge. Thankfully, they were able to prevent him from doing so and brought him to safety. However, that was not the last time Dor was instrumental in saving a man's life.

A year later, on a freezing winter night's walk in Iwade, Japan, Dor suddenly began to bark loudly and refused to continue on their walk. Instead, she went over to a metre-deep irrigation ditch and continued barking. Her persistent barking led Koichi to the ditch, where he realised what Dor had found.

There lay an 86-year-old man, face up and submerged in water up to his ears. Koichi pulled him out immediately. Since it was already dark and the temperature was so cold, it would have been very unlikely for the man to have been discovered before freezing to death if it hadn't been for Dor passing by and pinpointing his location with her amazing skills of perception.

Koichi then flagged down a passing car. As good fortune would have it, the driver was a doctor, who took the elderly man to his nearby practice and treated the injuries the man had sustained in the fall, which turned out to be only minor wounds to his hands and head.

The man made a full recovery, and Koichi was later awarded with a certificate of gratitude from the police for saving the man's life. A police officer commented that the certificate went to Wada because there was no precedent for awarding it to a dog, but clearly Dor was the hero of the day.

FOXY

Many elderly people who live alone like to keep pets for company. But one night in 2003, Joan Maguire discovered just how important a faithful companion can be...

Foxy, a pit bull cross, had been run over by a car and suffered a broken leg as a result. She had been operated on and recovered at the Little Shelter in Huntington, New York, USA but as a seven-year-old dog who needed daily supplements for her leg injury, and as a part pit bull (a breed that has a bad reputation), it looked as though no one would ever adopt her.

Eventually, however, 82-year-old Joan Maguire met her and it was love at first sight; Joan took Foxy home and they soon settled into life together. No one could have guessed how much of a blessing Foxy would prove to be to the elderly woman.

Joan was leaving her house one freezing evening to take Foxy for a walk when she slipped on the icy steps outside her house and fell, landing awkwardly. She tried to get up, but her leg wouldn't move and she lay helpless on the frozen ground, becoming colder by the minute. She tried signalling to her neighbours with her torch but no one noticed it and she began to panic, growing desperate as she realised that if she wasn't found before nightfall, she could die of exposure or hypothermia in the sub-zero temperatures.

Foxy realised that her owner was in pain and unable to move, so she spread her body across Joan's prostrate form in order to keep her warm. Then she began to bark to attract attention. But no help came for well over an hour. Undeterred, Foxy continued to bark, until a neighbour came outside to investigate the disturbance and quickly called an ambulance. Joan was taken into hospital and treated for a broken hip.

The old saying goes that an animal once rescued never forgets the one who saves its life. Foxy had certainly repaid her owner's kindness, and she was honoured with the ProHeart® Hero Award from Fort Dodge Animal Health.

PROHEART®
HERO AWARDS

The ProHeart® Hero Award programme was set up by Fort Dodge Animal Health, with the aim of honouring dogs who demonstrate heroism through acts of courage. The first award was presented to the New York Police Department

Canine Unit in January 2002 in recognition of their contribution at the World Trade Center disaster site. Other winners include Kaiser, a male German shepherd who saved his family from a fire in their home; and Bullet, a male golden retriever who alerted his owners when their baby stopped breathing.

MILLIE

A vigilant Border collie's early-morning barking led to the capture of four thieves in the act of breaking into the local post office...

When ten-year-old Border collie Millie wouldn't stop barking in the early hours one Saturday morning in April 2016, her owner Jane Partridge initially came downstairs to tell her to be quiet and then went back to bed. But Millie wouldn't give up, and when her owner looked out of her bedroom window to see what it was that had riled her dog, she saw burglars by the window of Ladock Post Office and immediately called the police, who arrived at 3 a.m. and caught the four thieves red-handed. They were arrested but released on bail pending trial.

Jane Partridge said:

> *If she hadn't woken me up I would not have heard them. Millie was a hero and I was*

making a lot of fuss of her that night. She
is very protective of us as a family and will
always let us know if someone has walked
past the house.

Tracy Mack, who runs the post office in Cornwall, UK, treated the Partridges to Sunday lunch at the local pub and thanked Millie, her saviour, with a gift of dog treats.

She said: 'It could have been so much worse if Millie hadn't woken up Jane.'

CHAPTER 10

KEEPING THE STREETS SAFE

Police dogs play a huge role in fighting crime – a role that is acknowledged by titles conferred all around the world on heroic police dogs. One such award is the Police Dog of the Year Award, granted annually by the Norfolk Constabulary in the UK to the winning dog chosen by the public from a number of nominees.

Police dogs carry out a wide range of duties. Their primary function is to protect their handler and enable them to carry out their job safely. In addition, they can act as a deterrent, and tracking dogs are used to locate a suspect who has fled. Search dogs can help find missing people; drug-detection dogs sniff out narcotics; bomb dogs can detect explosives; and other dogs specialise in sniffing out dead bodies or illegal weapons.

Many police dogs live at home with their handlers and become part of their family, and as a result the bond between handler and animal can become very strong indeed. As some of the following stories show, these dogs can be so dedicated to their protective role that they are willing to risk their own life in order to keep their handler safe.

IVAN

*You can run but you can't hide from the
nose of a highly trained police dog!*

After a high-speed car chase involving police officers in pursuit of two suspected drug dealers in Suffolk, UK, the suspects escaped when they abandoned their BMW and ran across a soggy field in the dead of night. The rain, lack of light and high grass of the field all stood in the suspects' favour, and, to the police officers, it looked like all might be lost.

But PC Simon Hughes and his dog Ivan weren't about to give up. The dog handler told the other police officers to return to their cars to avoid confusing Ivan with too many smells, and then took the sniffer dog over to the suspects' car.

After an hour of searching during which Ivan had shown no signs of interest in anything around the car, suddenly he pulled PC Hughes off into the waterlogged field and towards a river.

The field was covered in water from recent heavy rain, and it only got deeper the closer they got to the river. As they approached the reed beds of the river itself, the police dog became highly excited, leading Hughes to believe that he had detected someone close by.

He was right: there were two men in the reed bed, up to their knees in water, crouching down and silent in an effort to evade detection.

PC Hughes immediately identified himself and his dog to them, but despite this and the fact that Ivan was still barking at them, one of the men threw a punch at the policeman – at which point Ivan took control of the situation, biting the suspect's arm and then immediately releasing it.

That was enough for both men to become compliant and give themselves up. They were arrested and cannabis was found on both of them.

They might well have got clean away, though, if it hadn't been for the amazing tracking ability and quick protective action of the highly trained police dog, who was nominated for the 2016 Police Dog of the Year Award for his crime-fighting role that evening.

RHINO

A highly skilled police dog was nominated for an award for his crucial role in saving the life of an extremely vulnerable old man who went missing…

Police dogs are not only used for catching criminals. Their highly sensitive sense of smell and their incredible tracking ability means that they are regularly called upon to find missing people – who are often among the more vulnerable members of society, such as elderly people or those with mental health issues.

Police Dog Rhino, a highly skilled German shepherd dog, and his handler PC Martin Didwell of the Norfolk Constabulary, UK were involved in just such a case when an old man, who was suffering from depression and had previously attempted suicide, had not taken his medication and had gone missing.

The pair had been searching for him in vain in various areas for 29 hours, when suddenly Rhino tugged Martin towards a field full of very high wheat. Martin knew that his dog was onto something and after a brief search they located the injured man lying in the overgrown wheat, completely hidden from sight, and by then very weak.

The police officer immediately administered first aid and called for help, and the man was taken to hospital.

Rhino was nominated for the 2016 Police Dog of the Year Award – one of the Norfolk Constabulary's NOSCAs (Norfolk Safer Community Awards) – for his part in saving the life of a man who, had it not been for Rhino's amazing tracking ability, might easily have not been found until it was too late.

THE NOSCA AWARDS

Since 2014, the Norfolk Constabulary has included among its NOSCA (Norfolk Safer Community) awards a Police Dog of the Year Award in recognition of exceptional acts of bravery or devotion to duty shown by the force's police dogs with their handlers in any of three areas:

🐾 Diligence in detecting drugs, weapons, cash and stolen property.

🐾 Operational bravery in searching, tracking and detaining wanted people and resolving violent public order situations.

🐾 Searching for and saving the lives of vulnerable, missing people.

LUCAS

A fearless K-9 dog came to a police officer's rescue after he walked into a trap...

On his rounds in the southern state of Mississippi, USA, in May 2015, Deputy Todd Frazier pulled over to check up on the driver of a parked car at the side of the road who looked like he had passed out. As the officer walked over to the vehicle, he realised too late that it was an ambush, as two men leapt out at him from the bushes, and the driver got out of the car to join them. They grabbed his legs and started bundling him into the nearby woods, telling him they were going to slit his throat. One of them choked him, while another cut a gash in his forehead with a razor.

During the chaos, Frazier managed to get one hand free to reach a button on his belt that released his 34-kilogram

Belgian Malinois police dog Lucas from his police car. Lucas rushed towards the men, biting one of them and hanging on to his leg as the three of them tried to get back to their car to escape.

Officer Frazier said: '[Lucas] knew. I could hear him coming. I couldn't see anything because the blood was all in my eyes, but I could hear him coming, growling and making these sounds... he sounded like a wolf I thought, "Now he's gonna get you."'

The men eventually got away, but although Lucas, who has also located drowned bodies using his powerful sense of smell, ended up with all four of his canine teeth broken, a torn ligament, a bruised shoulder and road rash, neither his nor Frazier's injuries were life threatening.

Following widespread concern over Lucas's well-being following the attack, the Hancock County Sheriff's Office put out a notice assuring the general public that although he was still recovering from his injuries, the heroic dog was expected to make a full recovery – and had even had dental work to fix his teeth!

TRACER

Tracer, a German shepherd police dog, proved to be an invaluable member of the team when dealing with a dangerous armed man...

On the night of 26 September 2000, Corporal Joe Arduini and two other officers from North Vancouver Royal Canadian

Mounted Police were called out to deal with reports of a man carrying a gun. They approached the scene, stopping two blocks away from the location of the armed man, who was walking in their direction. Constable Christina Hughes and her dog Tracer were called in as backup and sent in closer to observe the man's behaviour. As Hughes was not in uniform at the time and the car she was driving was not marked as a police vehicle, she was able to do so without attracting the man's attention.

Hughes saw that the man was still advancing towards the three officers and was carrying a semi-automatic gun, so she radioed ahead to warn her colleagues. Arduini and his men acted fast, moving in to surround the suspect and instruct him at gunpoint to drop his weapon. When the suspect refused to comply, Hughes sent Tracer in to subdue him. Tracer did as all police dogs are trained to do in such a situation, and bit the armed man on his left arm. Normally this would have been enough to discourage a suspect, but this man didn't seem to feel any pain from the bite. With Tracer's jaws firmly clamped around his arm, he lifted the dog up in the air and back down, and then pointed his gun at the dog's head. As the officers looked on in horror, he pulled the trigger.

However, luck was on Tracer's side – the gun misfired and the dog was called safely back to Hughes' side. The suspect then turned the gun on the officers, forcing them to open fire in self-defence. He was fatally shot.

Tracer's fearless action that day in the face of life-threatening danger enabled the police officers to evaluate the suspect's unpredictable state of mind and take action before he hurt anyone.

KIAH

A rescued stray pit bull proved that she had all the qualities needed to be the first of her breed to become one of New York State's elite K-9 working police dogs...

When a highly trained pit bull was offered to various police departments at no cost to them, the police dog training agency (Universal K9) were sadly unsurprised that most departments didn't want to take her on, owing to the unfair reputation pit bulls have acquired as a vicious breed. But the City of Poughkeepsie in New York State, USA agreed to take her, noting her remarkable confidence – despite her poor start in life – as well as her intelligence, her natural curiosity, and her ability to concentrate on one thing – such as her beloved tennis ball! – to the exclusion of everything else going on around her. Had she been nervous, she would not have been able to cope with the stresses and distractions of life as a working police dog.

So in 2016, K-9 Police Dog Kiah became Officer Justin Bruzgul's first canine partner. The pair completed an initial 16 weeks of training in Texas, allowing Kiah to work as a patrol dog, followed by a six-week course in narcotics detection.

Although she became a prized member of New York State's highly trained K-9 unit – the first pit bull to belong to the unit – Kiah had originally been rescued from a supermarket car park as a stray suffering from a serious head wound. But the past was firmly in the past as far as she was concerned – of no relevance whatsoever to her current life in the police force. So successful was she in her new job that the director of operations for the Universal K9 training school rated her as among the top three dogs he had ever placed.

In her work keeping the streets of Poughkeepsie safe by helping to detect drugs and track missing people – as well as in serving as a goodwill ambassador for the police department – Kiah has more than repaid the favour of having been rescued from the dog shelter!

DID YOU KNOW?
ALL POLICE DOGS WORKING FOR CENTRAL SCOTLAND POLICE ARE REGISTERED BLOOD DONORS.

A cocker spaniel admitted to Broadleys Veterinary Hospital in Stirling, Scotland was suffering from anaemia and had a very low red blood count.

'The dog was so ill that the only chance of survival was to carry out a blood transfusion,' said Sergeant Cameron Shanks of the police dog section.

Luckily, the veterinary service was able to call upon Zak, a working police dog with the local force, for the blood donation necessary to carry out the transfusion. The cocker spaniel's life was saved and it was returned safely to its owners.

BRONX

A highly trained police dog gave chase to a
burglar, finally tracking him to his capture...

It was like a chase scene from an action-packed crime film – a policeman and his dog scrambling over a succession of 6-foot-high fences from one back garden to the next in an exhausting effort to catch a prolific burglar.

PC John Harwood and his dog Bronx from the Norfolk Constabulary had given chase following a burglary in the Norfolk town of Dereham, UK where thieves had made off with a large amount of stolen property.

The chase took them through woodland – where they found a laptop and other stolen property abandoned in some undergrowth near a tree – and carried on through the town itself and eventually into a cul-de-sac, which led to the pursuit over the fences.

Bronx, naturally good at jumping, relished this part of the operation, with his handler struggling behind him until they reached a spacious rear garden with a large conservatory.

It was at this point that Bronx, a highly trained sniffer dog, began barking at the conservatory door, alerting PC Harwood to the presence of someone hidden inside. It turned out to be the prolific burglar, who was arrested. PD Bronx and PC Harwood could return to base satisfied with their successful day's work! What's more, Bronx was nominated for a NOSCA Police Dog of the Year 2016 award from the Norfolk Constabulary for his fearless action.

ANYA

Neil Sampson and his K-9 partner Anya had only been working together for six months when the pair faced a violent and frightening situation...

Police Constable Neil Sampson is a dog handler with the Wiltshire Police, stationed at the Force Dog Section in Devizes, UK. In mid-2007, he was assigned a new dog to work with – Anya, a two-year-old German shepherd. She had only just finished her training as a police dog, and was very inexperienced, but she and Neil seemed to work well together and they had a good relationship. In early 2008, they were on their way to another job when a call came over their radio to attend to an incident nearby involving a man with a knife.

They headed straight to the scene, where other officers were already in attendance and talking to the person who had called the police. Neil decided to keep watch on the entrance to the flats where the incident had taken place, so that the man wouldn't be able to leave. The following is taken from Neil's report on the incident:

> *I had been watching the entrance to the flats for a short while when I saw a man leaving the block and start walking away from them and me. The male was of such appearance that I called out to him, which resulted in him turning round and walking towards me. As the male was approaching I called out*

*to him in an attempt to ascertain where he
had been; he did not reply, but at this point
I noticed what appeared to be blood on his
trousers, which made me believe he was
probably the male I was looking for.*

As the man didn't look aggressive, Neil didn't feel threatened by him walking towards him. The other officers were still talking to the first man, a short distance away. When Neil looked back towards the suspect, he suddenly realised that the man was carrying a knife. Neil asked him firmly to stop, but the man paid no attention and continued to walk towards him. As she was trained to do, Anya began to bark loudly and strain on the lead that Neil was holding. Usually this frightens a suspect enough to make them back off and cooperate. In this case, though, the man kept coming, slashing the knife in front of him as he did. Suddenly, the man began to attack Neil with both the knife and with his fist, punching and stabbing at him. Neil released Anya, who jumped at the man and bit him repeatedly, barking and growling as she did so. The man slashed at Anya with his knife and she fell back, then picked herself up and carried on trying to defend Neil.

*I have only a slight memory of the incident
after this point, I remember taser and PAVA
[police methods of subduing violent people]
being deployed and both failing to affect the
male, then feeling a pounding on the back
of my head and realising I was face down
on the ground and hearing the sounds of a
violent struggle taking place around me. I
was not aware that I had been stabbed but*

> soon became aware that I had been injured
> when, attempting to open my eyes, I found
> that one eye would not open and saw blood
> all around me; also, despite my best efforts
> to get up from the ground, I found that I was
> unable to.

The man had violently attacked Neil and Anya, slashing and lunging at them in a frenzied assault, and Neil was stabbed seven times in the back of the head and the legs, causing severe injuries. Another officer was also stabbed in the face whilst trying to help him. Eventually other officers from the armed response group were able, with Anya's help, to restrain the attacker and arrest him.

Anya had suffered a serious stab wound to her chest, which needed emergency surgery under general anaesthetic, but she made a full recovery from her injuries. Neil also recovered, but his injuries could have been far worse had it not been for brave Anya's intervention. The following is an extract from the armed response officers' report:

'It is the recollection of both officers that Anya remained focused on the offender, inflicting injuries that would subdue any normal person, however due to intoxicants and drugs taken by the offender, it is believed no pain inflicted could be felt and immense strength was gained.'

Anya's bravery had not only been a major part of apprehending and subduing a dangerous and violent criminal – who was later convicted on several accounts of violence, including a charge of criminal damage against Anya – but had also been instrumental in saving the life of her handler and in preventing any other officers from sustaining serious injury. Considering she had only been working as a police dog for six months and had never come across a violent situation like this before, her bravery and dedication to Neil were remarkable. The armed response officers' report contains a particularly poignant comment on Anya's courage, which demonstrates how grateful police officers are for the heroism of their dogs:

'Her presence and assistance on this day and during the incident assisted greatly in ensuring injuries caused were minimised, and without her presence and determination 'to not let go and to protect' it is felt undoubtedly that the outcome could have been sadly very different.'

As a result of the incident, Anya was honoured with the ACPO Police Dog Team Operational or Humanitarian Action of the Year Award 2008 at the Crufts Friends for Life Competition, arranged by the Kennel Club. In 2009, she was shortlisted for *The Sun*'s Hero Dog Award at the Dogs Trust Honours.

BESS

Ted Wright and his police dog, Bess, worked together as a team for many years. In that time, Bess was often called upon to help search for missing people...

Police officer Ted Wright and German shepherd Bess were called to Chatham, Kent, UK to help search for an 84-year-old lady named Elizabeth, who had been reported missing from a nursing home. Staff at the home were unable to find her when they tried to call her for lunch, so they notified the police. By evening, it was clear that the lady had indeed gone missing and the search team were alerted. The search was due to begin the next morning, so Ted and Bess set off very early to avoid the other search teams – it was easier and more effective for Bess to search unhindered by the presence of other officers.

They searched in gardens, alleys, rough ground, sheds and outhouses – anywhere in the immediate surroundings of the home to which the lady may have been able to gain access – but they had no success. Ted decided to do one last sweep of the area allocated for members of the public to search before nightfall. He recounts:

'There was one alleyway that was completely separated from the nursing home by a very high wall. Access to it was from an adjoining street, although it was never used and was overgrown with thick brambles, nettles and rubbish that had been thrown over the wall.'

Ted let Bess off her chain and asked her to search the alley, although he was not confident of any success in the dense undergrowth – he assumed the elderly lady would not have been able to make her way through the stubborn brambles. Soon Bess was working her way steadily through the alley, thorns tearing at her coat and skin. Ted followed, cursing and untangling himself every few steps. Suddenly, Bess gave signs that she could smell something. Ted told her to lead him to the source of the smell and they increased their pace through the brambles. Ted recalls:

> We had come to a sort of clearing that had a
> tree or two overhanging the path and there,
> where Bess was indicating, was the elderly
> lady, lying under a bush. She had obviously
> been there for some time. I crashed through

*the remaining brambles and told Bess to lie
down while I checked her condition. I asked
her some questions, but her replies came
only as moans. I used the radio to direct the
paramedics into the clearing, and the lady
was taken away in an ambulance.*

The nursing staff had been informed of the successful outcome of the search and Ted and Bess were treated to tea and biscuits back at the home, which they drank as they pulled the thorns from their clothing and fur. Elizabeth had a check-up at the nearby Medway Hospital and was released soon afterwards to return to the nursing home. The staff reported that she looked tired but fit, and hadn't suffered any ill-effects. It was never discovered how she managed to get into the overgrown alley. By the time she was located by Bess she had been missing for around 27 hours – any longer and it could have been a very different end to the story.

Ted would not have seen the lady, hidden by the bush that had also sheltered her from the overnight dew, if Bess had not barked at her to let him know she was there. Her sharp sense of smell had located the lady's scent from some distance, and she had known where to look when she arrived at the clearing. The lady was entirely obscured from human view, and it is thanks to Bess that she survived to tell the tale of her ordeal.

JAKE

*A dog that had an inauspicious start in life
later went on to become a fully trained
police dog and save a woman's life...*

At seven weeks old, Jake, a German shepherd, was left tied to a lamp post where he was tormented by young children with fireworks. He was taken in by the Northumbria Police, and with lots of loving care and training he had qualified as a police dog by his first birthday.

When he was three years old, he successfully located a 39-year-old missing woman who had collapsed deep inside a clump of bushes near Harton Cemetery in South Shields, South Tyneside, UK. Thankfully, she had only been missing from her home for an hour when the dog found her. The woman was taken immediately to hospital by emergency services.

'The fact the woman was found so quickly undoubtedly saved her life, as she was so deeply hidden you could barely tell she was there,' said PC Alistair Cairnie-Coates, Jake's handler. 'If she had been found much later, there could have been terrible consequences.'

CHAPTER 11

SURVIVORS!

Whether they're managing to make it through a brutal attack by humans or other animals, finding a way to hunker down and get through a disaster, coming through major surgery, or being helped back from the precipice by gentle rescuers, one thing is clear throughout the selection of stories in this chapter: dogs have an incredibly strong survival instinct – as well as, in the case of many dogs rescued from abusive situations or from a life spent fending for themselves on the street, the merciful ability to put their traumatic past behind them and get on with their happier lives in the present.

MARIA

A pregnant and paralysed miniature dachshund was found abandoned, terrified, and in urgent need of an expensive life-saving procedure...

Dachshunds, while comical, cute and appealing, do not have the best design and as a result need to be handled particularly carefully. Their long bodies and short legs mean that many suffer from back problems such as ruptured discs that leave them paralysed and in need of expensive surgery.

That was the case with Maria, a miniature dachshund living in Texas, USA, whose callous owners, greedy for the large sums of money they knew dachshund puppies could fetch, deliberately bred from her despite the fact that she was paralysed from the ribs down.

When they discovered that, being paralysed, Maria could only give birth by Caesarean section, which would cost $3,000, they simply abandoned their heavily pregnant pet.

That was when, thankfully, Friends of Emma stepped in. The charitable organisation with the mission to rescue and heal homeless and abandoned dogs in Texas took Maria in off the street and put up the money for her operation, in the process saving not only her life but the lives of her seven healthy puppies.

As well as being heavily pregnant when she was rescued, Maria was found to be severely anaemic from a severe and untreated flea infestation, and she also had a number of infections, in addition to carrying the emotional scars from having been neglected by her previous owners.

Miraculously, though, the tough little dog, who had got used to dragging her lifeless back legs behind her, learned to walk again in her safe new surroundings, even if a tad shakily. Homes were quickly found for most of the pups, while a very special new owner was sought for Maria herself, a happy, loving girl despite having had the worst possible start in life.

MOLLY, SILVA AND CHILLI

A succession of miniature dachshunds in one woman's life, each with an equally incredible story of survival, led her to invent her own wise saying: 'Once you go dax, you never go back!'

Mandy's first dachshund found her when she was living in Austin, Texas, USA back in 1998. The truth was, they found each other – Mandy found Molly wandering along the road looking painfully thin and missing the end of her tail, so she took her to work, put up posters in an attempt to locate her owner, and then joyfully kept her when no one came forward. And Molly, a true survivor of the streets, found Mandy at a time when she was quite low, picked her up, and made the trip across the Atlantic with her when she moved back to the UK two years later.

Mandy was devastated when she lost Molly in 2008 – by then an elderly girl with multiple health issues – and lasted ten months in her resolve not to get another dog. All she could think of was the heartache that having a pet brings at the end, forgetting all the joy they bring before that. But then she found herself scanning dog rescue sites and driving out to local animal shelters, feeling that there was an empty hole in her life in need of filling... And that's when Silva found her.

Silva was a two-year-old silver dapple miniature dachshund who had never been socialised and wasn't considered a good mother, and as a result was no longer wanted by the callous breeder, who had treated her purely as a money-making machine. She bonded immediately with Mandy, and life was good again for the two of them.

However, Silva's survival instincts would be put to the test not once but twice in the next few years. In 2012, overnight she was suddenly unable to walk, and it turned out she had a ruptured disc. An MRI scan and delicate surgery were the only option, but fortunately for Mandy, her pet insurance covered the expensive treatment.

Silva, by then aged six, came through the surgery in good shape and, after a month of cage rest, had to learn to walk again – and that's exactly what the determined little dog did, step by agonising step, and eventually life returned to normal for the pair... until, in December 2013, while she was out walking on her lead one day with her owner, poor Silva was badly attacked by a large dog that was off the lead. The dog pounced on her, shaking her neck and tearing a ligament, leading to severe blood loss and nearly the loss of her life.

Mandy had a chilling sense in the worrying hours that followed, when Silva underwent emergency surgery, of how fragile life is and of how she'd have nothing left if her beloved dog didn't make it through. At the same time, by pure chance, a friend contacted her from Wales about another miniature dachshund who had been rescued from a puppy farm where she had been used as a breeding bitch, and who now needed a forever home.

Happily, Silva did pull through, and two weeks later, she and Mandy made the journey down to South Wales to meet Chilli, a golden tan, lovely natured girl, remarkably unscarred by her previous life as a breeding machine – apart from suffering from an untreated hernia, the result of her teats being over-suckled. She bounced into Mandy and Silva's lives just before Christmas of 2013, and she and Silva instantly became fast friends and companions for life.

Three dogs, three stories of survival, and in this case, thankfully, three happy endings – as well as one happy human, besotted with her long-bodied, squatty-legged beloved girls!

DID YOU KNOW?
DACHSHUNDS ARE ESPECIALLY PRONE TO PROBLEMS WITH THEIR BACKS AND HIND LEGS

This is because of the length of their spines in proportion to their stumpy little Queen Anne–style legs. As a result, it's quite common for dachshunds to suffer from ruptured or herniated discs, leaving them paralysed all the way back from the damaged disc. But these tough little characters are also among the most adept at using specially designed wheels that replace their paralysed hind legs.

One such dachshund was Daisy who, at the age of six, was paralysed as a result of four herniated discs, and had ended up in a rescue centre. A developer of these specially designed wheels adopted Daisy to find out more about the needs of disabled dachshunds.

With Daisy on board as their eager test pilot, Eddie's Wheels went on to develop a range of attractive and functional wheeled carts, as with her help, they were able to learn a lot about how having a set of wheels enables a dog to progress from total paralysis to 'spinal walking' – that is, using their back in place of their hind legs.

Spunky little Daisy lived to the ripe old age of 16, remaining active and healthy right up until the stroke that ended her remarkable life.

ZIGGY

This young Staffordshire bull terrier was brutally shot through the head with a crossbow and left for dead...

Three-year-old Ziggy, a Staffordshire bull terrier, was dumped in a woodland near Peterborough in the UK after being callously shot through the head at point-blank range in a nearly lethal crossbow attack in October

2014. Luckily for Ziggy, he was found by a passer-by and taken to vet Cees Bennett, who said: 'X-rays revealed that the bolt had deflected off the exterior of his skull, miraculously missing all vital blood vessels, nerves, his eye and his ear canal – it was a one-in-a-million chance that he survived.'

Ziggy's brave spirit wasn't quashed by his terrible ordeal, and his tail continued to wag even as he arrived in the operating theatre to undergo delicate surgery to remove the bolt. Incredibly, within a few days of the operation he was discharged to boarding kennels, where he was soon swamped with offers of a forever home by dog lovers across the country who had heard his story. In the end he was adopted by Dominic O'Hare and Anna Burtonwood from Watford, who nominated him for the PDSA Pet Survivor Award 2015, which he won after thousands voted for him.

Dominic said: 'Ziggy is such an incredible dog – despite everything he's been through, he's still incredibly trusting and affectionate. We are absolutely overwhelmed that he's won the public vote to be named PDSA Pet Survivor 2015 – it's a tribute to his amazing survival spirit.'

MIA

When the family house was burning down around her and she was trapped inside, a young Belgian Malinois did the only sensible – and truly life-saving – thing, and headed for water!

The survival instinct well and truly kicked in when a young Belgian Malinois dog found herself trapped in a burning house all on her own. One-year-old Mia managed to prise open four doors to make her way to the basement, where she sat in a bathtub as it filled with water from the sprinkler system that had been set off by the blaze in the family home in South Carolina.

It took 30 firefighters two hours to control the blaze that was thought to have started in the attic while the family – Chris and Codi Brumby and their two children – were having a meal out.

Because the internal structure of the house made it unsafe to enter, it was six hours before the firefighters reached Mia, who had steam coming off her coat by the time she was eventually rescued.

When their beloved pet was brought out of the smoking wreckage alive, the family were overjoyed.

'That was a pretty special moment for us, because she's definitely part of the family,' said Chris Brumby.

Other than being dazed and covered in soot, miraculously she was otherwise unaffected by the traumatic incident that totally destroyed the house and could so easily have had a tragic ending.

LUNA

*When a young German shepherd–husky cross
vanished off a fishing boat into a wintry sea, the
odds were firmly stacked against her survival...*

After an 18-month-old dog disappeared off her owner's fishing boat two miles out to sea in February 2016, and no trace of her had been found after ten days of searching, her owner (a San Diego fisherman) posted photos of his dog on Facebook, accompanied by the sad message 'RIP Luna'.

Nick Haworth had been hauling in a catch when the blue-eyed German shepherd–husky cross disappeared overboard. With the help of the US Navy, he searched the waters for two days and San Clemente Island lying two miles offshore for a week, but to no avail.

Nearly five weeks after she had vanished, however, Luna was found sitting on the US Navy-owned island, San Clemente, by navy personnel who worked there. Apart from being thinner, the courageous young dog was no worse for her ordeal. She must have reached the island by swimming the two miles to shore, although it is not known how long she spent in the water before reaching the island's safe haven.

After he was reunited with his fortunate pup, Nick then posted another, much happier entry on Facebook. It read:

'Beyond stoked to have Luna back. I always knew she was a warrior.'

FRIDA

An injured German shepherd survived in the middle of a busy freeway for an incredible five weeks before finally being rescued...

When a German shepherd fell off the back of a truck onto a California freeway in April 2016, and disappeared, obviously injured, into the thick oleander bushes growing on the median dividing the northbound and southbound lanes of traffic, there was a wave of concerned calls to the local police department from motorists who'd witnessed the distressing incident.

But although the police from Galt, a city in Northern California, were sent to look for the dog, who was sighted several more times over the next few days, no one was able to catch her before she vanished again. And then the calls tailed off.

But early one morning five weeks after the dog had fallen from the truck, another sighting came in from a motorist who had spotted her on the highway.

That was when Galt Police Officer Sylvia Coelho stepped in and decided that it was time to find the dog once and for all. She had rescued animals all her life and was a huge dog lover, having been devastated when her late father's dog, that she had taken in, passed away.

Her fellow officer Christina Hill was the first to spot the injured dog – nicknamed Agent 99 by the police, but referred to in the newspaper and TV reports as Freeway Frida. Another officer arrived, and eventually the three of them were able to round up the terrified animal, blocking her path onto the busy freeway if she bolted.

Frida initially put up some resistance to being captured, but 45 minutes later she seemed to give up the fight and submit to being caught. By then she was severely emaciated, weighing half what she should have. How she survived those five weeks on the freeway median is unknown, though she probably drank the scant rainwater that collected there and found small amounts of food by foraging in the bushes.

Five-year-old Frida was checked over by the vet at the local animal hospital, who found that she had a fractured tibia and fibula and tendon damage that might not ever fully heal. Meanwhile, the police switchboard was flooded with calls from people wanting to adopt the by now famous dog who had survived against all the odds.

However, the following month Police Officer Coelho took Frida home with her – to join her chihuahua and three cats – so strong was the bond that had developed between the two of them since the day of her rescue!

KALU

A stray dog was found with most of his face missing – yet still with the will to live. But could he recover from such a severe wound?

If ever there was a dog who demonstrated an indomitable spirit and an incredible ability to survive, it's Kalu.

The stray, whose face had been almost completely eaten away by maggots, had crawled into a construction site hole in India to die in excruciating pain when he was discovered by charity workers in 2015.

Determined to help the poor creature, who appeared to have lost both his eyes as well as his nose, they contemplated euthanasia as the only way of putting him out of his suffering. But there was something about the severely injured dog that made them think again – a spark that was still there and that cried out for a chance at life.

So what was left of his face was treated with a powder that killed the maggots and fly larvae, and then he was anaesthetised so that the terrible wound could be cleaned and bandaged.

No one knew whether recovery was possible from such a devastating injury... but there was a flicker of hope when on the third day after his surgery, the injured dog they had named Kalu began to eat. And on the fifth day a miracle happened – his left eye, that had initially appeared to have been lost to the infestation, suddenly reappeared – and he could see through it!

Gradually the facial wound began to heal, new flesh grew back on the exposed skull, and new hair appeared on the flesh.

A mere three months after he had nearly been given up on, Kalu was filmed bouncing around with a new and joyful spring in his step.

Other than missing one eye and his tail, Kalu is now a healthy dog, and he has a contented life at the Animal Aid Unlimited shelter in Udaipur, Rajasthan, whose shocked workers had found him in such a pitiful state only a few months previously.

ARTHUR

When a Swedish extreme sports team set off on a gruelling race through the Amazonian rainforest, little did they know that they'd end up taking on an extra team member along the way – in the form of a mangy, yet determined, stray dog!

When, in 2014, extreme athlete Mikael Lindnord, a member of Team Peak Performance, showed a little kindness to a hungry stray dog by tossing him a meatball during a rest stop in Ecuador on an early stage of the 430-mile Adventure Racing World Championship, he thought nothing more of it – until it became clear that the little mutt had latched on to the Swedish team and wouldn't be shaken off, come hell or high water!

The dog, named Arthur by the team, took on every demanding task that the team faced during their participation in the physically demanding race, swimming next to their kayaks, trotting alongside them on their challenging jungle treks, and dragging himself up steep hills in order to remain by their side.

He became so much part of the team that when Mikael saw him struggling in the water during a 36-mile leg of the race on the river, he pulled him on board his kayak, and there Arthur remained for the duration of the leg.

The team started taking rest stops to allow the little dog to catch his breath on their exhausting hikes, and fed him cans of their precious supplies of food when he was unable to find enough food on his own. When the extreme race finished after six days, it was apparent that Arthur was in pain as a result of his dogged determination to stick by the team, so they took him to a local vet to have his injuries treated.

By then, Mikael realised that he had become so bonded to Arthur that he couldn't just abandon the little stray who had become his friend, and so he applied to the Swedish Board of Agriculture *(Jordbruksverket)* for permission to take Arthur home with him.

An agonising wait followed while a decision was made – and Mikael was overjoyed when he received word that he could go ahead and take Arthur back to Sweden.

Mikael wrote a book in 2016 called *Arthur: The Dog Who Crossed the Jungle to Find a Home*, and said, 'I came to Ecuador to win the World Championship. Instead, I got a new friend.'

GOBI

Like Arthur, a young stray dog faithfully stayed by the side of an athlete competing in an extreme marathon across China – and ended up with a new home in Edinburgh!

When Dion Leonard came second in a gruelling 155-mile marathon across China in June 2016, the prize that meant more to him was winning the heart of a stray dog who joined him at the start of the race and ended up crossing the finishing line in his arms.

Dion spotted the young dog, who he named Gobi, hanging around the camp the day before the six-stage week-long race began. He thought she couldn't have been more than 18 months old. During the race, temperatures reached 52°C, and Gobi was not allowed to take part in two of the stages because of the extreme heat. During the other stages, though, she would run ahead of Dion and then wait for him to catch up. Even though it slowed him down, he carried her across a stretch of river that was too wide for her to cross on her own, as by then their bond had become too strong to leave her behind.

Dion Leonard and Gobi had bonded so much by then that Dion decided he was going to do whatever it took to bring his new friend back home to Scotland with him. Within 24 hours of setting up a crowdfunding campaign on 27 July, considerably more than the £5,000 needed to reunite the pair had been raised. He planned to donate the excess amount to dog charities, and hoped Gobi would be home in time for Christmas.

Although Gobi would have to go through two lots of quarantine – in China and then again in Scotland – Dion and his wife Sarah were determined to bring the loyal little pup home.

Dion said: 'She really liked the cold weather of the Tian Shan mountain. She didn't like the heat much, so she'll be right at home in Edinburgh.'

DID YOU KNOW?
DIFFERENT BREEDS FEATURE
DIFFERENT DESIGN ELEMENTS

Some breeds of dog have inbuilt design elements that make them better than others at fending for themselves and making it through the tough times – although any breed of dog can be a wonder dog!

- The basenji, the oldest breed of dog, is a natural hunter and defender, and intelligent enough to silently (as it doesn't bark) outwit its competitors.

- The coonhound is bred for heartiness, intelligence and, above all, a keen sense of smell. Driven by instinct to form hunting parties, coonhounds are naturals at stalking their prey and outsmarting their enemies.

- The cairn terrier is a robust breed with a wiry outer coat that keeps it dry in the wettest of weather, and a dense, fluffy undercoat that keeps it warm through the depths of winter.

- The Newfoundland has the stamina to swim for days if necessary.

- The Alaskan malamute has a weather-proof double coat that protects it in even the most extreme climes. It is also a powerful, clever breed.

- The xoloitzcuintle (Mexican hairless dog) has a body that is the product of 3,000 years of evolution in Mexico's tropical climate, so it can survive in very hot conditions, and its survival instincts remain strong.

- The Fila Brasileiro was bred to hunt large jungle beasts – such as jaguars and boars – and as well as being a tireless hunter, it also has a powerful sense of smell.

ACKNOWLEDGEMENTS

Thank you to everyone who helped with gathering material and the research for this book, particularly Sister Janet Fearns, Katie Williams and Sue Pritchard. Special thanks go to Pam Williams at Norfolk and Suffolk Constabularies for Ivan, Bronx and Rhino's stories; Jane and Robbie Probets for Dougie's story; Steve Jamieson and Janeta Hevizi, Tamsin Thomas at RNLI and Sue Nicholls at Penwith District Council for Bilbo's story; Jon Hastie and Vicky Bell at the Guide Dogs for the Blind Association for Yaron's story; Karen Frith at Lake District Search Dogs for Dottie's story; Neil Hamilton Bulger and James Coles at Search and Rescue Dog Association Southern Scotland for Briar's story; Nicola Willis and Jenny Moir at Hearing Dogs for Deaf People for Lye's story; Gary Wickett and Vicky Bell at the Guide Dogs for the Blind Association for Roz's story; Lizzie Owen and Allie Hogsbjerg at Dogs for the Disabled for Bella and Frodo's story; PC Neil Sampson and Katie Whitworth at Wiltshire Constabulary, and Victoria Brown and Melinda Dziedzic at the Kennel Club for Anya's story; Ted Wright for Bess's story; and Mandy Woods for Molly, Silva and Chilli's story and Hannah's story.

USEFUL RESOURCES
AND INFORMATION

If you feel inspired by the stories in this book, you may be interested in finding out more about relevant charities and organisations.

Barry Foundation

As owner of the breeding kennels of St Bernard dogs since 2005, the Barry Foundation's responsibility is the preservation and continued management of the three-century-old breed at its place of origin.

+41 (0) 27 722 65 42
www.fondation-barry.ch

British International Rescue and Search Dogs (BIRD)

BIRD is a highly trained team of volunteers, based in North Wales. Their aim is to alleviate the suffering of victims involved in disasters at home and abroad, providing a rapid response service involving the use of search and rescue dogs.

+44 (0) 1248 681321
www.birdsearchandrescuedogs.co.uk

Canadian Avalanche Rescue Dog Association (CARDA)

This is a volunteer non-profit charitable organisation. Their aim is to train and maintain a network of highly efficient avalanche search and rescue teams across Canada.

www.carda.ca

Cancer and Bio-detection Dogs

This charity works in partnership with researchers from the Buckinghamshire Hospitals NHS Trust, who are supported by the charity Amerderm Research Trust. Their aim is to train specialist dogs to detect the odour of human diseases, including cancer and diabetes.

+44 (0) 1296 655888
www.medicaldetectiondogs.org.uk

Canine Epilepsy

The canine epilepsy website aims to help with the diagnosis and management of epilepsy, and also with the differentiation between epilepsy and other forms of seizure. The peer-reviewed information it contains has been provided by leading neurologists in the UK, and it also provides a comprehensive list of neurology specialists around the UK, as well as details of support groups.

www.canineepilepsy.co.uk

Canine Partners

Officially launched in the UK in 1990, Canine Partners enables people with disabilities to enjoy greater independence and a better quality of life through the help of specially trained dogs. Assistance dogs can transform the lives of people with disabilities by helping in practical ways such as dressing and undressing, supermarket shopping and vital emergency response procedures. In addition, they provide physiological, psychological and social benefits that help keep people healthy and happy.

+44 (0) 8456 580480
www.caninepartners.org.uk

Crufts

The world's largest international dog show is held annually in London, UK and organised by the Kennel Club.

www.crufts.org.uk

Dogs for Good (formerly known as Dogs for the Disabled)

An innovative charity set up in the UK in 1988, exploring ways dogs can help people overcome specific challenges and enrich and improve lives and communities. Its vision is of a world in which everyone and every community is able to benefit from the help of a trained dog.

+44 (0) 1295 252600
www.dogsforgood.org

Dogs Trust (formerly known as the National Canine Defence League)

The organisation was founded in 1891 'to protect dogs from torture and ill-usage of every kind'. It is the UK's largest dog welfare charity and cares for over 17,000 dogs each year through its network of 20 rehoming centres in the UK and one in Dublin. Its mission is to bring about the day when all dogs can enjoy a happy life, free from the threat of unnecessary destruction.

+44 (0) 207 837 0006
www.dogstrust.org.uk

Four Paws

Four Paws is an international animal welfare charity. Its vision is a world where humans treat animals with respect, empathy and understanding. Its mission is to be a strong, global and independent voice for animals under human control by creating sustainable solutions for animals in need, touching hearts, changing consumer behaviour, driving legal changes and building powerful partnerships. Its projects and campaigns provide short-term and long-term solutions for animals in need.

+44 (0) 20 7922 7954
www.four-paws.org.uk

Give a Dog a Home

This small not-for-profit organisation (eventually to become a charity), set up in 2013, rescues abandoned or street dogs from Greece, Romania, Cyprus and Spain and fosters them in specially selected homes in Sussex, Kent and Surrey in the UK, ready for adoption, again by carefully checked homes.

+44 (0) 7896 041561
www.giveadogahome.org.uk

Guide Dogs for the Blind Association (UK)

This organisation exists to provide guide dogs and other mobility services that increase the independence and dignity of blind and partially sighted people. It campaigns for improved rehabilitation services and unhindered access for those who are blind or partially sighted.

+44 (0) 118 983 5555
www.guidedogs.org.uk

Hearing Dogs for Deaf People

This is a UK-based registered charity that selects and trains dogs to respond to specific sounds. Hearing dogs alert deaf people by touch, using a paw to gain attention and then leading them back to the sound source. For sounds such as smoke alarms and fire alarms, the dogs will lie down to indicate danger. Whenever possible, the dogs are selected from rescue centres, but they are also donated by breeders and members of the public, with the remainder coming from the charity's own breeding scheme. The charity provides a national service and no charge is made to recipients. Since its inception in 1982, Hearing Dogs for Deaf People has placed more than 1,500 hearing dogs.

+44 (0) 1844 348 100
www.hearingdogs.org.uk

Hounds for Heroes

Hounds for Heroes was set up in 2010 to provide specially trained assistance dogs to injured and disabled men and women of both the UK Armed Forces and the Emergency Services. Through this provision, its aims are to provide help and practical support leading to an enhanced quality of life for its clients.

+44 (0) 1730 823118
www.houndsforheroes.com

Humane Society of the United States

This is the USA's largest animal protection organisation. Established in 1954, the HSUS seeks a humane and sustainable world for all animals.

+1 202 452 1100
www.humanesociety.org

International Hearing Dog, Inc. (IHDI)

IHDI has trained more than 950 hearing dogs since 1979 for persons who are deaf or hard of hearing. All of the dogs selected for this special training come from local animal shelters in the USA.

+1 303 287 3277
www.hearingdog.org

Kennel Club

The primary objective of the Kennel Club is to promote, in every way, the general improvement of dogs.

+44 (0) 1296 318540
www.thekennelclub.org.uk

Lake District Mountain Rescue Search Dogs

A voluntary UK-based organisation dedicated to the training and use of mountain rescue search dogs to assist in the search for and rescue of missing persons, predominantly in a mountainous environment, but also in other areas where their skills may be of benefit. All Lake District Mountain Rescue Search Dog handlers are also members of a mountain rescue team affiliated to the Lake District Search and Mountain Rescue Association (LDSMRA) and therefore must already be competent in first aid and survival in a mountainous environment. The association is a registered charity that can continue to exist only because of public donations.

www.lakes-searchdogs.org

Last Chance Animal Rescue

Last Chance Animal Rescue Centre is a registered charity based in Kent, UK, rescuing, rehabilitating and re-homing dogs, cats, rabbits and guinea pigs to most areas of the UK. They operate a no-destruction policy.

+44 (0) 1732 865530
www.lastchanceanimalrescue.co.uk

Many Tears Animal Rescue

Many Tears Animal Rescue (MTAR) is a small rescue based in South Wales but has dogs in foster homes throughout the UK. They take in and rehome primarily ex-breeding dogs who are no longer required; those on 'death row' in the pounds; and those whose owners are no longer able to keep them. MTAR also has a small cattery, enabling them to take a small number of cats.

+44 (0) 1269 843084
www.manytearsrescue.com

National Search and Rescue Dog Association (NSARDA)

The NSARDA is an umbrella organisation for Air Scenting Search Dogs in the UK. Its members are the Search and Rescue Dog Associations located throughout the UK. Each of the individual Search and Rescue Dog Associations (SARDA) is a voluntary organisation responsible for the training and deployment of air-scenting search and rescue dogs to search for missing persons in the mountains and high moorlands of Britain as well as the lowland, rural and urban areas.

www.nsarda.org.uk

Oldies Club

The Oldies Club works with animal rescues to publicise the plight of their older dogs. Its website lists oldies from hundreds of rescues around the UK.

+44 (0) 844 586 8656
www.oldies.org.uk

Oxfordshire Animal Sanctuary

The Oxfordshire Animal Sanctuary rescues and rehomes over 500 animals in the Oxfordshire area every year. Since opening in 1967 it has managed to help over 25,000 animals. Its aim is to ensure that no animal is forgotten about, providing abandoned animals with a second chance at finding a loving home.

+44 (0) 1865 890239
www.oxfordshireanimalsanctuary.org.uk

PDSA

PDSA is the UK's leading veterinary charity, caring for more than 350,000 pet patients belonging to people in need. They provide free veterinary treatment to sick and injured animals and promote responsible pet ownership.

+44 (0) 800 917 2509
www.pdsa.org.uk

Penrith Mountain Rescue Team

PMRT was founded in 1959 and is affiliated to the Lake District Search and Mountain Rescue Association (LDSAMRA) and to the national governing body, Mountain Rescue England and Wales (MREW). The team is manned entirely by volunteers who give freely of their time and skills to provide a search and rescue resource to Cumbria Constabulary. Their area of operation covers nearly 1,000 square miles across the Lake District National Park (north-eastern Fells), the northern Pennines and the Eden Valley.

www.penrithmrt.org.uk

The Seeing Eye

The Seeing Eye is the oldest existing dog guide school in the world. Twelve times a year, as many as 24 students at a time visit the campus in Morristown, New Jersey, USA to discover the exhilarating experience of travelling with a Seeing Eye dog.

+1 973 539 4425
www.seeingeye.org

SUPER CATS

TRUE TALES
of EXTRAORDINARY FELINES

ASHLEY MORGAN

SUPER CATS
True Tales of Extraordinary Felines

Ashley Morgan

£8.99

Paperback

ISBN: 978-1-84953-998-2

Meet the Super Cats:

Emily, the feline that survived an epic journey across the Atlantic trapped in a shipping container from America to France.

Scarlett, the brave mother that went into a burning building five times to rescue her kittens.

Oscar, the care-home cat that predicts when residents are about to pass on and comforts them in their final hours.

Whether they're testing the boundaries of their nine lives or demonstrating unusual talents, cats are always full of surprises. In *Super Cats*, prepare to meet the most surprising of all. Discover loyal moggies that put their lives at risk, intuitive cats that detected danger when no one else did and extraordinary feline survivors in this heartwarming collection of true tales.

ANIMAL
HEROES

True Stories of
Extraordinary Creatures

Ben Holt

ANIMAL HEROES
True Stories of Extraordinary Creatures

Ben Holt

£8.99

Paperback

ISBN: 978-1-78685-005-8

Meet the Animal Heroes:

Magic, the miniature pony who helped a woman speak again after three years of silence

Stubby, the stray dog who braved the front line with soldiers in World War One

Moko, the bottlenose dolphin who guided a mother whale and her calf back out to sea

No matter how cute and cuddly our animal companions are, there are always occasions when they remind us that they're still in touch with their natural instincts. Sometimes this comes as little gestures of loyalty, and other times they do something that is truly amazing – even saving human lives.

Animal Heroes contains some of the most extraordinary true tales of bravery across the natural world, from domestic pets to wild animals, proving that when it comes to facing danger there's more to them than meets the eye.

My Rescue Dog
Rescued Me

Amazing true stories of
adopted canine **heroes**

Sharon Ward Keeble

MY RESCUE DOG RESCUED ME
Amazing True Stories of Adopted Canine Heroes

Sharon Ward Keeble

£8.99

Paperback

ISBN: 978-1-84953-950-0

Meet the inspirational dogs who went from being rescued to becoming rescuer, in these incredible true stories.

You'll read all about...

Toby, the golden retriever who performed the Heimlich manoeuvre to save his owner's life

Liam, the Lhaso Apso–Poodle mix who helped his owner battle an eating disorder

Hercules, the St Bernard who saved his owners from burglars on the first day he moved in

Alfie, the terrier who gave a bullied girl a new lease of life

... as well as many other canine heroes who came to their owner's aid – whether it was saving them from physical threats, or helping them to recover from mental illness, PTSD and bereavement.

DOGS

A MISCELLANY

VICKY EDWARDS

DOGS
A Miscellany

Vicky Edwards

£9.99

Hardback

ISBN: 978-1-84953-736-0

This pocket-sized miscellany – packed with doggy facts, stories of the world's most impressive canine feats and famous mutts from literature, history and art, and tips on looking after your pooch – is perfect for anyone who values the trusty companionship of their favourite hound.

Have you enjoyed this book?
If so, why not write a review on your
favourite website?

If you're interested in finding out more
about our books, find us on Facebook
at **Summersdale Publishers** and
follow us on Twitter at **@Summersdale**.

Thanks very much for buying this
Summersdale book.

www.summersdale.com